PREFACE

This global survey, based entirely on open sources, is intended to provide an assessment of the nexus between selected anti-U.S. terrorist and extremist groups in the world and organized crime, specifically drug trafficking, and how this relationship might be vulnerable to countermeasures.

More specifically, the aim is to help develop a causal model for identifying critical nodes in terrorist and other extremist networks that can be exploited by Allied technology, just as counterdrug technology has been used in the war against drug trafficking. To this end, the four analysts involved in this study have examined connections between extremist groups and narcotics trafficking in the following countries, listed by region in order of discussion in the text: Latin America: Triborder Region (Argentina, Brazil, and Paraguay), Colombia, and Peru; the Middle East: Lebanon; Southern Europe (Albania and Macedonia); Central Asia: Kyrgyzstan, Tajikistan, and Uzbekistan; and East Asia: Philippines. These are preliminary, not definitive, surveys.

Most of the groups examined in this study have been designated foreign terrorist organizations by the U.S. Department of State. The exceptions may be the small Albanian insurgent groups and the Central Asian organization called the Hizb-ut-Tahir (HT). These groups are included anyway because of their links to al Qaeda and narcotics trafficking, as well as because of their potential for terrorism.

Although research was begun on groups in Egpyt (al-Gama'a al-Islamiyya and Islamic Jihad), Somalia (Al-Ittihad al-Islamiya), South Africa (People Against Gangsterism and Drugs–PAGAD), and Yemen (Islamic Army of Aden), insufficient information was found on links with the drug trade to merit further investigation, given the time constraints of this research project. In the cases of PAGAD and al-Gama'a al-Islamiyya, however, further research may be warranted because the possibility of involvement with the narcotics trade cannot be ruled out.

TABLE OF CONTENTS

KEY POINTS

- As a result of the significant decline in funding of guerrilla and terrorist groups by ideologically motivated state sponsors since the end of the Cold War, these groups have become increasingly reliant on drug trafficking as a principal funding source.

- Indigenous guerrilla and terrorist groups operating in drug-producing regions of Afghanistan, Colombia, Peru, and elsewhere are heavily involved in the drug trade.

- In most cases, the relationship between insurgent groups and drug-trafficking organizations or cartels is a mutually beneficial one that allows exchanges of drugs for weapons, use of the same smuggling routes, use of similar methods to conceal profits and fund-raising, e.g., informal transfer systems such as the *hawala* and the Black Market Peso Exchange (BMPE), use of the same resources for laundering money, use of the same corrupt government officials, and so forth. However, the cartels and the drug-trafficking terrorist and extremist groups have different goals: the former are primarily motivated by financial enrichment and do not seek attention, whereas the latter, because of their political goals—or, in the case of the Islamic groups, both religious and political objectives—are more likely to receive close attention by the public and by law enforcement authorities. As a result, the insurgent groups and the drug cartels have a pragmatic, arm's-length relationship.

- The terrorist and extremist groups derive much of their drug-related income from taxation levied for protection of drug growers, laboratories, clandestine landing fields, and transport of drugs or precursor chemicals through guerrilla-controlled territory.

- The Islamic fundamentalist groups are known to be increasingly involved in drug trafficking to fund their operations and to further the degradation of Western society. Documentation of the extent of their involvement, however, is lacking.

- Almost all of the terrorist/extremist groups identified as being involved in narcotics trafficking also reportedly have had contacts with al Qaeda, which is known to be actively engaged in drug-trafficking activities.

- "Charitable" and other non-governmental front organizations are used by worldwide terrorist organizations, such as al Qaeda and Hizballah, to channel funds to their affiliated terrorist groups. The Saudi-based International Islamic Relief Organization (IIRO) is an example.

- As some insurgent groups have become increasingly involved in the drug trade, their criminal enterprises have assumed greater priority than their own ideological, political, or religious agendas. Examples include the Abu Sayyaf Group (ASG) in the southern Philippines and the Revolutionary Armed Forces of Colombia (FARC) in Colombia.

INTRODUCTION

Growing Worldwide Links Between Narcotics Trafficking and Terrorist/Extremist Groups

The connection between narcotics trafficking and insurgent groups and networks has been fairly well documented in recent years. Rand Beers, the U.S. deputy assistant secretary for international narcotics and law enforcement affairs, and Francis Taylor, the U.S. Department of State's ambassador-at-large for counterterrorism, told a U.S. Senate panel on March 13, 2002, that terrorist groups have increasingly turned to drug trafficking as a source of revenue as heightened international efforts have diminished the funding role of state sponsors.[1] According to the two officials, the move into drug trafficking also has a secondary strategic, purpose: "Not only does it provide funds, it also furthers the strategic objectives of the terrorists. Some terrorist groups believe that they can weaken their enemies by flooding their societies with addictive drugs."[2]

During the Cold War, state sponsors such as the Soviet Union and its allies, including Cuba, provided funding and other support for terrorist organizations. Since the collapse of the Soviet Union and its East European allies and the end of the Cold War, state sponsorship of terrorism has come under greater international scrutiny and condemnation. International pressure against Islamic terrorist and extremist groups in particular and state sponsors of terrorism in general increased dramatically after al Qaeda's terrorist attacks against the World Trade Center and the Pentagon on September 11, 2001. Governments have interdicted terrorist finances and shut down "charitable" and other non-governmental front organizations used by terrorist groups. Traditional state sponsors of terrorism, such as Cuba, Iran, and Libya, have come under growing

---

[1] Rand Beers, Assistant Secretary for International Narcotics and Law Enforcement Affairs; Francis X. Taylor, Ambassador-at-Large for Counterterrorism, "Narco-Terror: The Worldwide Connection Between Drugs and Terror," a hearing held by the U.S. Senate Judiciary Committee, Subcommittee on Technology, Terrorism and Government Information, March 13, 2002.
[2] Ibid.

international (particularly U.S.) pressure not to aid terrorists, and Cuba has not had the funds to do so even if it wanted to.

The decrease of state sponsorship of terrorism in the 1990s led to a concomitant increase in efforts by terrorist groups to become self-financed through drug trafficking. In his September 1995 address to the United Nations, President William Clinton highlighted the dangers of transnational organized criminal activity and cited the "the growing nexus between terrorists, narcotics traffickers and other international criminals that has been fostered by developments in international communications, travel and information-sharing, and the end of the Cold War."

Increasingly, terrorist and drug-trafficking organizations have been using similar methods to conceal profits and fund-raising. These include informal transfer systems such as the *hawala* and the Black Market Peso Exchange (BMPE) (see graphic in Venezuela section). Former U.S. Internal Revenue Service (IRS) official Alvin James explained to the U.S. Senate Committee on Banking, Housing, and Urban Affairs on September 26, 2001, that terrorists use the BMPE's $5 billion in annual funds transfers as a cover for hiding the movement of terrorist funds. James added:

> What is more, the 1993 terrorist attacks on the Twin Towers were financed at least partially with funds that were moved through this market. That money is ready for those who need a discreet source of funds that is difficult to trace.... The links to terrorist funding through the BMPE are even stronger today since the placement of drug dollars into U.S. financial institutions now begins in any country of the world.

The BMPE is active in Colombia, Dominican Republic, Guatemala, Haiti, and Venezuela. In these countries, the system is linked to Israel, Lebanon, Palestine, and Australia.

About half of the 28 groups officially designated as terrorist organizations by the U.S. Department of State are believed to have ties to drug trafficking. In Latin America, these groups include three in Colombia: the left-wing National Liberation Army (Ejército de Liberación Nacional—ELN) and Revolutionary Armed Forces of Colombia (Fuerzas Armadas Revolucionarias de Colombia—FARC), and the right-wing United Self Defense Forces of Colombia (Autodefensas Unidas de Colombia—AUC). Also on the list of narcoterrorist groups in Latin America is Peru's Shining Path (Sendero Luminoso—SL). Colombian and Peruvian insurgent and paramilitary groups that are involved in coca production exert control over regions containing coca fields, laboratories, and airstrips and impose taxes ranging from $100 to $500 per kilogram to protect the area.

Beers has argued that FARC involvement goes beyond protection of drug cultivation areas and laboratories to include the transportation of drugs and chemical precursors and even direct control of its own laboratories. He also asserts that the FARC and the ELN "are receiving pure cocaine in payment for services provided to the drug traffic, and reselling it" to Brazilian criminal organizations in return for armaments. The FARC, in particular, operates in league with Brazilian, Colombian, and Mexican drug cartels.

Increasingly, terrorist organizations flush with drug funds have been establishing a presence in North America. According to a November 2001 report by Royal Canadian Mounted Police (RCMP), South American drug shipments entering Canada are a potential source of terrorist funds.[3] Up to 25 tons of cocaine, worth as much as $50 million, arrive in Canada annually.[4] According to the RCMP intelligence report, proceeds from lucrative Asian hashish shipments smuggled into Canada likely ended up in the hands of "terrorist elements in Afghanistan." According to police, most of the more than 100 tons of hashish reaching the Canadian market each year originated in Afghanistan and Pakistan. "Most of the documented hash importations have been with southwest Asian suppliers that have been in this business for 10 to 20 years," the RCMP report says. "It is likely that terrorist elements in Afghanistan tax producers, thereby receiving a portion of the potential proceeds." Canadian traffickers have paid an average of US$200 per kilogram to brokers in these countries, meaning about $20 million has found its way back to producers annually. East Indian, Afghan, Pakistani, Tamil, Turkish, and Middle Eastern terrorist or extremist groups are "suspected of fund-raising in Canada by various means," the report adds. But the RCMP suggests that further investigation is needed to confirm suspicions of Canadian links between terrorists and drug traffickers.

Narco-terrorist groups in Europe include the Basque Fatherland and Liberty (Euzkadi Ta Azkatasuna—ETA) from Spain's Basque region. Reporting indicates that the ETA or its

---

[3] "RCMP: Hash Cash Aids Terror Cells," *Montreal Gazette*, February 16, 2002, A10, citing the *Southam News*, which obtained a copy of the declassified November 2001 criminal intelligence report, *Narcoterrorism and Canada*, under the Access to Information Act.
[4] Ibid.

members have been involved in a variety of crimes, from drug trafficking to money laundering. There is some evidence linking the Real Irish Republican Army (IRA) to the Middle Eastern narcotics industry. However, the extent to which the Real IRA or other terrorist groups in Ireland engage in drug trafficking is unclear. This study, however, has found links between drug trafficking and former guerrillas of the Albanian Liberation Army (KLA). The KLA spin-off groups are well positioned to exploit the Balkan Route, which links the Golden Crescent of Afghanistan and Pakistan to European drug markets. As of 2002, Albanian liberation extremists had reportedly used profits from their participation in Taliban-sponsored narcotics smuggling to re-arm themselves.

Activities of the Kurdistan Workers' Party (PKK) have also included laundering money and drug trafficking.[5] Beers, speaking at a meeting on narcoterrorism held by the Technology, Terrorism and Government Information Subcommittee of the U.S. Senate Justice Committee, said that the PKK had taken protection money from drug traffickers and supported their own operations with the revenue gained.[6] Speaking at the same hearing, the administrator of the U.S. Drug Enforcement Administration (DEA), Asa Hutchinson, noted that the PKK is involved in the taxation of drug shipments and the protection of drug traffickers throughout the Southeastern Region of Turkey.

In the Middle East, Hizballah is increasingly involved in drug trafficking, according to Beers and Taylor. Hizballah smuggles cocaine from Latin America to Europe and the Middle East and has in the past smuggled opiates out of Lebanon's Beka'a Valley, although poppy cultivation there has dwindled in recent years. According to analyst Frank Cillufo, in 2000 Hizballah was reportedly cooperating with the PKK to export narcotics into Europe.[7] Beers, Cillufo, Taylor, and others seem to believe that Hizballah's involvement in drug trafficking and other illicit activity may expand as state sponsorship declines, but that currently Hizballah is still reported to be receiving substantial funding from Iran. This study found that Hizballah has been sending multi-million dollar amounts from the Triborder Region to Canada, Lebanon, and elsewhere. However, in contrast to the charges made by Beers, Cillufo, Taylor, and others,

---

[5] Mircea Gheordunescu, "Terrorism and Organized Crime: The Romanian Perspective," *Low Intensity Conflict & Law Enforcement*, 11, No. 4, Winter 1999, 26.
[6] Beers.
[7] Frank Cillufo, "The Threat Posed from the Convergence of Organized Crime, Drug Trafficking, and Terrorism." Statement before the U.S. House Committee on the Judiciary, Subcommittee on Crime, December 13, 2000.

conclusive information documenting alleged Hizballah involvement in narcotics trafficking was not found.

In Central Asia, DEA statistics indicate that, in 2000, before the Taliban imposed a poppy-cultivation ban that greatly reduced the size of the 2001 harvest (see chart), Afghanistan produced 70 percent of the world's opium poppies, which are the source of heroin. The Taliban's poppy-growing ban had a minimal effect on world drug markets, however, because the Islamic fundamentalist regime of Mullah Mohammed Omar had been stockpiling as much as 65 percent of previous years' harvests, according to DEA spokesperson Will Glaspy.[8] After the ban helped to drive up the world price for heroin, the Taliban then sold from its reserves, getting a higher price, according to Glaspy.

After being refined in laboratories in Afghanistan and Pakistan, the heroin is smuggled abroad, mostly to Western Europe and Russia. Only a small percentage of Afghan heroin came to the United States, where the heroin sold on the streets reportedly comes mainly from Colombia and Mexico. Until the Taliban was deposed in the fall of 2001, the illicit drug trade in Afghanistan was long considered a primary source of money for the Taliban. In turn, the

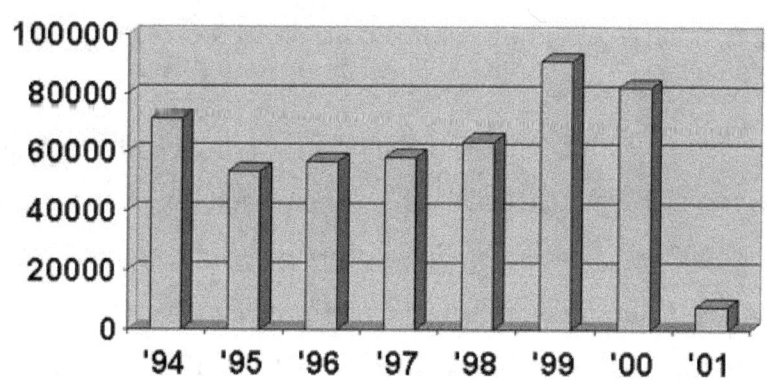

Opium Poppy Cultivation in Afghanistan, 1994-2001

In Hectares

Source: "Opium Poppy Cultivation in Afghanistan, 1994-2001," United Nations International Drug Control Programme (UNDCP), *Afghanistan: Annual Opium Poppy Survey 2001.*

Taliban hosted Osama bin Laden, whose al Qaeda terrorist network is suspected of selling protection to traffickers. In his congressional testimony on March 13, 2002, DEA's Hutchinson

---

[8] Mary Jacoby, "War's New Target: Drugs," *St. Petersburg Times*, February 11, 2002.

noted that DEA had received multisource information that bin Laden has been involved in the financing and facilitation of heroin trafficking activities.[9]

One of the Central Asian groups spawned by bin Laden's al Qaeda is the Islamic Movement of Uzbekistan (IMU), a militant Islamic organization. This study has found that the IMU funds itself largely from drug trafficking, and that the IMU controls the main drug-trafficking routes through the Central Asian region. According to *Jane's* analyst Tamara Makarenko, the IMU has diverted security forces by engaging them in armed clashes on the southern borders of Uzbekistan and Kyrgyzstan during the summer months because of the IMU's role in narcotics trafficking.[10] Shipments of Afghan narcotics are especially heavy during the summer months, and the main trafficking routes for them run through the Pamir Mountains of Tajikistan.[11] In 2000 the IMU stored at least 1,500 tons of narcotics in the Tavildara district of northern Tajikistan, according to official estimates.[12] Makarenko also points out that areas penetrated by the IMU—the Surkhandarya and Batken regions—host many known trafficking routes.[13] According to Makarenko, "...the key to success in fighting the IMU primarily lies in the region's ability to control the growing drugs trade through their territory—this, however, will depend on the situation in Afghanistan."[14]

Elsewhere in Central Asia, the Kashmiri militant groups are likely to participate in the drug trade to finance their activities, given their proximity to major production and refining sites and trafficking routes. Throughout the South Asia and former Soviet Union regions, proximity to cultivation and production, combined with the infrastructure provided by the traffickers, has also encouraged mutually beneficial relationships between terrorist groups and drug-trafficking organizations. Individual members and sympathizers worldwide of the LTTE in Sri Lanka traffic drugs, principally heroin, to raise money for their cause. The LTTE reportedly has close ties to drug-trafficking networks in Burma (also known as Mayamar), and Tamil expatriates may carry drugs in exchange for training from Burma, Pakistan, and Afghanistan. The United Wa State

---

[9] Prepared testimony of Asa Hutchinson before the Senate Judiciary Committee Subcommittee on Technology, Terrorism and Government Information hearing on "Narco-Terror: The Worldwide Connection between Drugs and Terror."
[10] Tamara Makarenko, "Terrorism and Drug Trafficking Threaten Stability in Central Asia," *Jane's Intelligence Review*, 12, No. 11, November 2000, 29.
[11] Ibid.
[12] Ibid.
[13] Ibid.
[14] Ibid, 30.

Army (UWSA) controlled major drug-producing areas in Burma and used the proceeds to carry out an insurgency against the government of Burma until a ceasefire agreement granted the UWSA enough autonomy to continue drug trafficking for profit. The Wa have also engaged in large-scale production and trafficking of synthetic drugs. In Southeast Asia, this study has found links between narcotics trafficking in the region's Golden Triangle and the Abu Sayyaf Group (ASG) in the Philippines.

Growing Involvement of Islamic Terrorist and Extremist Groups in Drug Trafficking

Increasingly in recent years, Islamic terrorist and extremist groups have turned to drug trafficking as a source of revenue, rationalizing their involvement as a strategic necessity not only for their existence but also as a way to weaken the enemy. An overview of the rise of the Islamic fundamentalist movement may provide some context for understanding its role in the narcoterrorism nexus.

By far the most extensive terrorist network operating in the world today is the Islamist International that Iranian intelligence reportedly initiated in the early 1990s.[15] According to author Jossef Bodansky, its terrorist and militant arm came to be known as the Armed Islamic Movement (AIM), a.k.a. International Legion of Islam. Its terrorist vanguard is known as the Afghans—those who trained with the mujahideen in Pakistan or fought against the Soviet Union in Afghanistan. As Bodansky explains, "Since the early 1990s, the Islamist Legion has been sending its mujahideen all over Asia, Africa, Europe, and the United States to support, further, incite, and facilitate what the leadership considers Islamic liberation struggles."[16] He adds that affiliated Islamist groups and organizations are active all over the world wherever Muslims live, and that Islamist terrorists operate out of bases in Afghanistan, Iran, Pakistan, and Sudan. By 1992, according to Bodansky, the AIM, under the sponsorship of Pakistan's Inter-Service Intelligence (ISI) agency, was supporting and training "Islamist terrorists and fighters for jihads throughout the world from centers in Afghanistan and Pakistan."[17] He explains further that, "As a result of the growing cooperation between the various Islamist movements, they had

---

[15]Jossef Bodansky, *Bin Laden: The Man Who Declared War on America* (Roseville, California: Prima Publishing/Random House, 2001), 34.
[16] Bodansky, 35.
[17]Ibid, 49.

established an "International Jihad Organization" using Pakistan and Afghanistan as their springboard to the rest of the world."[18]

Although often described as operating in loosely organized, autonomous small cells, the Afghans, Bodansky points out, "actually constituted a global unifying factor because they brought the organizations and movements they had joined into the Islamist fold."[19] By 1996, with assistance from the ISI, the Islamist terrorist infrastructure in Afghanistan had been consolidated, Bodansky says.[20] In early October 1997, under the direction of the ISI and bin Laden, who shuttled between Afghanistan and Tehran, "major preparation began in Afghanistan and Pakistan for an escalation of Islamist terrorism throughout the world," according to Bodansky.[21] In 1998 Islamist networks throughout Europe and the Middle East activated "a large, diverse system for clandestine travel by terrorists…from North Africa, the Middle East, the Balkans, and Western Europe to and from Pakistan, Afghanistan, and to a lesser extent Yemen."[22]

A bin Laden representative, Mohammad Jamal Khalifa, began recruiting Filipino fighters for the war in Afghanistan as early as 1988.[23] The recruits included dozens of Muslims from the island province of Basilian and many others from elsewhere in the southern Philippines. According to another source, Khalifa, bin Laden's brother-in-law, flew from Jeddah, Saudi Arabia, to Manila, the Philippines' capital, that year to establish a branch of the Saudi-based International Islamic Relief Organization (IIRO).[24] According to Philippines' intelligence officers, the IIRO office and an array of associated business ventures have been used to channel funds to the ASG.[25] This study has provided additional evidence that several bin-Laden-linked charitable foundations in the Philippines have been used as conduits for funding the Moro Islamic Liberation Front (MILF) and the ASG.

According to author Simon Reeve, World Trade Center bomber Ramzi Ahmed Yousef met Khalifa and ASG founder Abdurajak Abubakar Janjalani in Peshawar, Pakistan, in the

---

[18]Ibid, 50.
[19]Ibid, 52.
[20]Ibid, 186.
[21]Ibid, 209.
[22]Ibid, 347.
[23] Simon Reeve, *The New Jackals: Ramzi Yousef, Osama bin Laden and the Future of Terrorism* (Boston: Northeastern University Press, 1999), 157.
[24] Mark Huband, "Bankrolling bin Laden," *Financial Times*, November 28, 2001.
[25] Ibid.

summer of 1991, and bin Laden began actively providing financial support to the ASG at that time.[26] Also on that occasion, Khalifa persuaded Yousef to travel to the Philippines to train ASG terrorists. Yousef subsequently visited the Philippines on behalf of bin Laden.[27] In August 1994, again at the request of bin Laden's officers in Pakistan, Yousef again traveled to the Philippines to train ASG terrorists in the use of sophisticated high explosives.[28] After several weeks of training more than 20 Abu Sayyef terrorists on the island of Basilian, Yousef moved to Manila that September, until fleeing the country on January 7, 1995, after police searched his Manila apartment.

In the early 1990s, bin Laden sent Afghan Arabs into Albania and then into Bosnia to fight in battles between Muslims and Serbian aggressors in the neighboring former Yugoslavia. After the Bosnia Peace Accord was signed in Dayton, Ohio, in 1995, many of the Arab Afghans in the region moved to Kosovo. By the spring of 1999, "al Qaeda was still well established in Albania," according to Reeve.[29] Reeve points out that bin Laden retained a large investment in the Islamic Bank in Tirana, and that "…Sheikh Claude Ben Abdel Kaden, a French national of Algerian extraction, has traveled the country recruiting young Muslim militants for al Qaeda."[30]

According to Bodansky, "The support and management echelons of the new Islamist networks operate in conjunction with organized crime."[31] Bodansky explains that Iranian intelligence agencies first encouraged Islamic radical groups to participate in the drug trade. Since then, the Islamic terrorist and extremist groups have expanded into myriad criminal activities, to include, in addition to drug trafficking, operating prostitution rings involving mainly Bosnian Muslim and North African women, laundering money, and disseminating high-quality, Iranian-printed $100 bills. He points out that Hizballah's original fatwa, issued in the mid-1980s, on the distribution of drugs, has provided a rationale for drug trafficking:

> We are making these drugs for Satan—America and the Jews. If
> we cannot kill them with guns, so we will kill them with drugs.

The Islamic terror network is not likely to give up using guns to destroy America and its Western allies. The increasing use of the same smuggling routes by terrorist groups and drug-

---

[26]Reeve, 136, 156.
[27]Ibid, 158.
[28]Ibid, 71-2, 158.
[29]Ibid, 211.
[30] Ibid, 211.
[31] Bodansky, 322.

trafficking organizations could have serious national security implications. As Tom Riley, spokesman for the Office of National Drug Control Policy, explained, "If you wanted to smuggle bombs into America, there is a ready-made network to do that. It is the drug network."[32] Canada and Mexico, sharing long borders with the United States, provide easy access and escape routes for terrorists. Numerous foreign terrorist groups, such as the Liberation Tigers of Tamil Eelam (LTTE) from Sri Lanka, are known to have branches in Canada. By the late 1990s, numerous foreign terrorist groups were also known to have established themselves in the United States. These include the Abu Sayyef Group, al Qaeda, the Egyptian Ga-mat Islamiya, Hamas, Hizballah, Hizba-Tahrir (the Islamic Liberation Party), the Islamic Jihad, Jamat Muslimeen (from Pakistan and Bangladesh), and the Taliban.[33] As the al Qaeda affiliate, Armed Islamic Group (GIA), demonstrated in December 2000, when it attempted to smuggle components for a powerful bomb into Washington State from Canada, al Qaeda and its other affiliated terrorist organizations can be expected to attempt to smuggle increasingly deadly weapons into the United States, possibly using drug-smuggling routes.

NARCOTICS-FUNDED TERRORIST/EXTREMIST GROUPS IN LATIN AMERICA

Key Points

- Indigenous guerrilla/terrorist and paramilitary groups operating in drug-producing regions of Colombia and Peru are heavily involved in the drug trade.
- These groups derive much of their drug-related income from taxation of drug growers and drug traffickers.
- Increasingly, insurgent and paramilitary groups in Colombia are using cocaine and opium to barter for weapons and other materiel from the drug cartels, particularly the Russian mafia.
- In most cases, the relationship between Colombian and Peruvian insurgent and paramilitary groups, on the one hand, and drug-trafficking organizations or cartels, on the other, is a mutually beneficial one that allows exchanges of drugs for weapons, use of the same smuggling routes, use of similar methods or resources for laundering money, use of

---

[32] Mary Jacoby, "War's New Target: Drugs," *St. Petersburg Times*, February 11, 2002.
[33] Reeve, 232, citing Steven Emerson's prepared statement delivered before the Senate Judiciary Subcommittee on Terrorism, Technology and Government Information, February 24, 1998.

the same corrupt government officials, and so forth. However, the cartels and the drug-trafficking terrorist and extremist groups have different goals—the former are primarily motivated by financial enrichment, whereas the latter have political or, in the case of the Islamic groups, religious goals. As a result, they have a pragmatic, arm's-length relationship.

- If the large amounts of funds being sent by Islamic fundamentalist groups in Latin America to bank accounts in Canada, Lebanon, and elsewhere are any indication, these groups may be increasingly involved in drug trafficking in the region to fund their worldwide operations and to further the degradation of Western society.

- In the absence of adequate documentation, however, it cannot be assumed that these large amounts of money are derived from drug trafficking. The Islamic fundamentalist groups operating in the region are also heavily involved in extortion of Arab or Muslim business people, smuggling of contraband and weapons, and Black Market Peso Exchange (BMPE) operations.

- Various Islamic fundamentalist groups have been operating out of the Triborder Region. These include the shadowy al-Muqawamah (the Resistance), which has a base in the region, and reportedly is linked to Hizballah and Iran.

ISLAMIC FUNDAMENTALIST GROUPS OPERATING IN LATIN AMERICA

Introduction

Approximately 6 million people of Muslim descent live in Latin America. In addition to Argentina and Brazil, there are Muslim communities in Bolivia, Chile, Colombia, Honduras, Paraguay, and Peru. Extremist cells tied to Hizballah, Islamic Jihad, and al Qaeda are operating in Argentina, Ecuador, Honduras, Mexico, Nicaragua, Paraguay, Uruguay, and Venezuela, and pose a potential threat to U.S. businesses, military personnel, and civilians throughout the region. Although one of the first major acts of Islamic fundamentalist terrorism in the region may have been the bombing of the Israeli Embassy in Buenos Aires on March 17, 1992 (see below), another significant incident took place only four months later. On July 19, 1992, a suicide bomber said to be Lebanese and unable to speak Spanish or English boarded a commuter flight in Colón, Panama, and detonated a bomb, killing all 21 people aboard, including 12 Jewish and Israeli businessmen, and three U.S. citizens. The bomber was said to have a poorly forged U.S.

passport and to have not been in Panama very long. The next major act of Islamic fundamentalist terrorism in the region took place again in Argentina on July 18, 1994 (see below).

Since then, several additional planned acts of Islamic fundamentalist terrorism have been thwarted. For example, the arrest in 1998 of a senior Abu Nidal Organization (ANO) leader in Lima, Peru, thwarted a reported plan to blow up the Israeli Embassy and a synagogue there. According to O *Globo*'s U.S. sources, al Qaeda supposedly planned an attack against the U.S. Embassy in Montevideo, Uruguay, in April 2001, at the same time as a planned attack against the U.S. Embassy in Quito, Ecuador. The discovery of the plot (and the consequent reinforcement of security) thwarted the attacks.[34] Following the September 11, 2001, attacks, U.S. Central Intelligence Agency (CIA) and Federal Bureau of Investigation (FBI) agents reportedly traveled to Uruguay to investigate possible links with the bin Laden network.

Of particular concern to U.S. authorities since late 2001 is the possibility that lax immigration procedures in various Latin American countries have allowed terrorist "sleepers" to adopt new identities and to infiltrate into the United States, especially from Argentina. Tens of thousands of Argentines entered the United States under the visa-waiver program, and there is reportedly no documentation showing that they returned to Argentina.[35]

Islamic extremist support networks in South America are found in Colombia, particularly Maicao in La Guajira Department; Ecuador; Uruguay, particularly the town of Chui on the border with Brazil; the Triborder Region of Argentina, Brazil, and Paraguay; and Venezuela, particularly Margarita Island. Moreover, in addition to the U.S. border with Mexico, the porous borders of the Caribbean may potentially provide a strategic haven for terrorists, given the links among drugs, arms, and money laundering.

Hizballah clerics and members of other violent Islamic groups reportedly began planting agents and recruiting sympathizers among the Arab and Muslim immigrants in Latin America in the mid-1980s, at the

---

[34] "Brazil: Daily Notes US Views Triborder as Al-Qa'idah Center for L.A.," FBIS LAP20011029000036, October 29, 2001, translating Jose Meirelles Passos, "The Shadow of Bin Ladin in Latin America," *O Globo* (Rio de Janeiro; Internet Version-WWW), October 29, 2001.
[35] Martin Anderson, "Al-Qaeda Across the Americas," *Insight on the News*, November 26, 2002, 20-22.

height of the Lebanese civil war. Hizballah cells began to form in the Triborder Region as a result of Hizballah proselytizing in the Lebanese communities.

International law enforcement agencies have reported that radical Islamic activity in Latin America is closely connected to drug trafficking and arms dealing in the area, particularly in Colombia and in the Triborder Region. Islamic fundamentalist organizations such as Hamas, Hizballah, and Islamaya al Gama'at actively use the Triborder Region as a support base. For example, they use the region to raise revenues through illicit activities that include drug- and arms trafficking, counterfeiting, money laundering, forging travel documents, and even pirating software and music. In addition, these organizations provide safe havens and assistance to other terrorists transiting the region.

As early as 1995, Ambassador Philip Wilcox, former State Department Coordinator for Counter-Terrorism, testified before the International Relations Committee of the U.S. House of Representatives that Hizballah activities in the Triborder Region involved narcotics, smuggling, and terrorism. He further asserted that Hizballah also had cells in Colombia and Venezuela, was engaging in fund-raising and recruitment, and was receiving guidance and logistical support from Iranian intelligence officers assigned to Iranian embassies in the region.[36]

The Triborder Region: Sociocultural and Geographical Environment

The Triborder Region is a lawless jungle corner of Argentina, Brazil, and Paraguay with at least half million inhabitants. Its borders roughly consist of the Argentine port city of Puerto Iguazú, the Brazilian city of Foz do Iguaçu in Paraná State, and the Paraguayan city of Ciudad del Este. The region's most famous landmark is Iguaçu Falls in Paraná State.

Figures vary on the size of the Arab population in the Triborder Region. A 2001 *Jane's* article noted more precisely that 629,000 people, among them 23,000 Arabs of Palestinian and Lebanese descent, live in the Triborder Region.[37] Although only about 2,000 Arabs live in Ciudad del Este, they have considerable financial influence. According to some estimates, between 15,000 and 21,000 Arabs of Palestinian and Lebanese descent live and work across the Brazilian border in Foz do Iguaçu and its surrounding hinterlands, while maintaining commercial

---

[36] Ambassador Philip C. Wilcox, Jr., "International Terrorism in Latin America," Testimony to the U.S. House of Representatives, Committee on International Relations, September 28, 1995.
[37] John Daly, "The Suspects: The Latin American Connection," *Jane's Terrorism & Security Monitor*, October 1, 2001.

outlets in Ciudad del Este. Foz do Iguaçu, which is Brazil's largest Arab community, reportedly has 11,000 Muslim residents. Another Paraguayan city with a large Arab population and known as a main contraband center is Encarnación. Paraguayan antiterrorist police detained 16 mostly Middle Eastern foreigners for interrogation in Encarnación on September 21, 2001.

Paraguayan Police Sergeant Derci Barroso told Rio de Janeiro's daily *Jornal do Brasil* that members of the Arab community own properties scattered throughout Alto Paraná State, covering an area of 13,000 square kilometers. He explained that most Arab immigrants live in gated condominiums in Foz do Iguaçu, in Brazilian territory.[38] The sizeable and influential Arab community in this region may help to explain why the Lebanese government decided in January 1999 to close its embassy in Asunción, Paraguay, and to open a consulate in Ciudad del Este to watch over the interests of the Arab citizens.[39] Another reason was that nine representatives of Hizballah in Lebanon's Parliament requested the move.

Paraguay's Ciudad del Este, located 330 kilometers to the east of Asunción, is the capital of Upper Paraná State and the country's second largest city. Strategically located, Ciudad del Este is situated on the Pan American Highway, which runs from Asunción, Paraguay, to Curitiba in Brazil. The city has a population ranging from 170,000 to 250,000 by day, but many people leave at night to return to the Brazilian city of Foz do Iguaçu, where the quality of life is better than in Ciudad del Este. Foz do Iguaçu has a population of approximately 350,000 inhabitants. The population of Puerto

---

[38] "Argentina, Paraguay, Brazil Step Up Search for 'terrorists' in Triborder Area," BBC Monitoring Service [UK], September 15, 2001.

[39] "Arabic Factions 'Bidding' for New Lebanese Consulate," *ABC Color* [Asunción; a major daily opposed to the González Macchi administration], January 31, 1999, 61, as translated by FBIS, FTS199902001001342.

Iguazú, on the Argentine side, has been variously reported as low as 14,000 and as high as 35,000 people.

Like Casablanca during World War II, Ciudad del Este is an oasis for informants and spies; peddlers of contraband (largely cheap East Asian goods) and counterfeit products; traffickers in drugs, weapons, and humans (prostitutes, including women and children forced into prostitution); common criminals; mafias; undocumented Arabs; and terrorists. General Alberto Cardoso, chief minister of Brazil's Institutional Security Office, told *Correio Brasiliense* on November 8, 2001, that "There is smuggling, drug trafficking and money laundering in the Triborder Region. Those characteristics make the area a more favorable place for using laundered money to finance illegal activities, including terrorism."[40]

Despite a lack of tourist hotels, many tourists, mostly Brazilians, visit Ciudad del Este during the day to purchase cheap consumer goods. Since the region began receiving negative publicity in late 2001, at least 500 of Ciudad del Este's 12,000 registered businesses have gone out of business as a result of the reduced tourist trade.

The Triborder Region

The three principal cities in the Triborder Region

Arabic is heard as much as, or perhaps more than, Spanish in Ciudad del Este, which has three mosques. The city's Arab community is among Latin America's most prosperous and influential. The Arab community in the Triborder Region is tightly knit, with its own schools and clubs, making outside penetration very difficult. The high concentration of immigrants from the Middle East, especially in Ciudad del Este and Foz do Iguaçu, allegedly facilitates the activities

---

[40] "Brazil: Official Admits Triborder Money Laundering May End Terrorism," BBC Monitoring Service [UK], November 22, 2001, citing *Correio Brasiliense* web site [Brasilia], November 9, 2001.

of bin Laden's sympathizers. A few extremists may get together, form a cell with no risk of leaks, carry out their mission, and return with alibis backed up by many in the community.

In addition to Arabic, Chinese is also widely spoken in Ciudad del Este. The city's 5,000 Chinese, mostly from China's southern Canton region, prefer this city over Foz do Iguaçu. Some of these Chinese residents are connected to the Triad, a Chinese mafia.

The principal criminal activities in the Triborder Region are reported to be piracy of consumer products; falsification of identity documents; laundering of drug money; and smuggling of weapons, drugs, and stolen automobiles. Smuggling stolen cars is a booming business. Cars are stolen in Brazil and Argentina and taken to Paraguay, and then to Bolivia and beyond. According to Paraguayan authorities, more than half of the 450,000 vehicles registered annually in Paraguay were acquired illegally.

Many of the Brazilian tourists who visit the city during the day do so to buy contraband or counterfeit products at cut-rate prices. An estimated 90 percent of the products sold are counterfeit. U.S. authorities estimate the U.S. companies lost $117.1 million in 1996 in piracy of products in Paraguay. According to police in Brazil and Paraguay, it is easy to obtain a false passport, birth certificate, driver's license, and other documents through corrupt officials. "Anyone can buy a new identity and nationality here," Augusto Aníbal Lima, spokesman for Paraguay's National Police in Ciudad del Este, was quoted by AP on September 19, 1994. "Of all the Arabs in the area, only 273 are legally registered."

The Tancredo Neves (Friendship) Bridge across the Rio Paraná links the Brazilian border city of Foz do Iguaçu with Paraguay's Puerto Iguazú. Few of the estimated 30,000 to 40,000 people who cross the bridge every day are checked by the authorities.

With more than 100 hidden airstrips in the triangle, the region has always been a safe haven for gunrunners and drug traffickers. Arms exported officially from Brazil to other members of the Common Market of the South (Mercosur) are clandestinely reimported to Brazil through Ciudad del Este. Altino Remy Gubert, Jr., police chief in Foz do Iguaçu, told AP in

17

September 1994 that millions of dollars worth of sophisticated weapons arrive each year from Miami in sealed drums aboard cargo ships, which sail up the Paraná and unload arms in Ciudad del Este, where they are sold to Brazilian smugglers.

The Islamic Fundamentalist Presence in the Triborder Region: Background

Home to about 250,000 Jews, Argentina has Latin America's largest Jewish community, but the country's population of Arab descendants is about triple that number. Approximately 700,000 people of Muslim descent live in Argentina. These sociodemographic factors have made Argentina a prime target in Latin America not only for Islamist terrorism against Jews but neo-Nazi terrorism as well.

In the first half of the 1990s, Islamic fundamentalist terrorists in the Triborder Region carried out two major terrorist operations against the Jewish community in Buenos Aires. Islamic terrorists operating out of the Triborder Region leveled the Israeli Embassy in Buenos Aires with a powerful bomb on March 17, 1992, killing 29 people and wounding 252. The bombing was allegedly carried out by Hizballah and coordinated by terrorist mastermind Imad Mughanniyah (hereafter, Mugniyah) (alias 'Hajji'), the official in charge of Hizballah foreign operations. Using false Brazilian documents (in the name of Muce Sagy), a Syrian arms trafficker named Monzer Al Kassar was in Foz do Iguaçu to deliver explosives to the group headed by Lebanese Imad Mugniyah.[41] (In 1985 Monzer Al Kassar had pretended to be a Rio de Janeiro resident selling arms to Iranian militias on the island of Cyprus.)

On July 18, 1994, a car-bomb exploded at a Jewish cultural center, the Argentine-Israeli Mutual Association (AMIA), in Buenos Aires, demolishing the seven-story building and killing 84 and wounding 300 people. Mugniyah's Islamic Jihad, one of the armed branches of the pro-Iranian Lebanese Hizballah party, is also accused of having perpetrated the attack against the AMIA. Islamic Jihad claimed responsibility shortly after the attack. The Buenos Aires police

---

[41] "Conexão brasileira" [Brazilian Connection], OnLine Época, October 9, 2001.

gathered clues indicating that the explosives or detonators used in the 1994 AMIA bombing were taken from Foz do Iguaçu. Israel's Mossad intelligence agency held a Hizballah cell responsible for both attacks, saying they were orchestrated by Mugniyah, in cooperation with the Iranian intelligence service (see also Venezuela). The Israeli Embassy in Buenos Aires formally accused Mugniyah of providing the explosives used in the AMIA bombing. According to alleged U.S. and Israeli intelligence sources cited by *Insight on the News* magazine, Mugniyah was involved in the planning of the AMIA attack and may have parachuted into Argentina at the last minute to activate sleeper networks and handle logistics for the operation, subsequently escaping with the help of an Iranian diplomatic passport.[42]

Clarín published an Argentine intelligence report on the AMIA bombing as well as the report of the Argentine judge who was appointed to investigate the incident. The reports claimed that there were links between Iranian diplomats in Caracas and Hizballah cells throughout the South American region. *Clarín* also reported that Iranian diplomats provided terrorists with "logistical support, arms, and explosives, using the diplomatic pouch for such purposes."[43]

On August 25, 1995, Principal Superintendant Enrique Martinetti, chief of the Intelligence Department of the National Police, confirmed to *ABC Color* [Asunción] that three members of a Hizballah "sleeper cell"—Johnny Moraes Baalbaki, Luis Alberto Nader, and Mohammed Hassan Alayan—had been arrested in Paraguay for questioning about alleged terrorist activities. The three had arrest warrants out for them in Argentina for possession of explosives and suspicions of taking part in the bomb attack that destroyed the Israeli Embassy in Buenos Aires in March 1992.

---

[42] Kenneth R.Timmerman, "Likely Mastermind of Tower Attacks: Imad Mugniyeh," *Insight on the News,* 17, No. 49, December 31, 2001, 18-21.

[43] Edgar O'Balance, *Islamic Fundamentalist Terrorism, 1979-95: The Iranian Connection* (New York: New York University Press, 1997), 14-15.

After the AMIA bombing, Islamic fundamentalists reportedly began planning another terrorist attack, this time possibly against a U.S. target. A Hizballah leader, Ali Hussein Hamsa ("Imand Fakia"), was reported to have arrived in Argentina on November 15, 1995, but it was not reported whether he was connected to terrorist planning activities. On April 25, 1996, *El Territorio* [Posadas, Paraguay] reported that Superintendent General José Werner, chief of police of Misiones Province, had confirmed that 20 Hizballah suicide commandos were present in Ciudad del Este, and that they were able to complete their training in the Triborder Region. Confirmation of this report appears to be lacking.

In November 1996, it was discovered that Islamic groups in the Triborder Region were planning to blow up the U.S. Embassy that month in Paraguay to coincide with the first anniversary of the bombing of the Saudi National Guard headquarters in Riyadh, Saudi Arabia.[44] Details of the plot were revealed with the arrest of Marwan 'Adnan al-Qadi ("Marwan al-Safadi"), 40, who was linked to an Hizballah-affiliated group. Police who raided his apartment in Ciudad del Este found it filled with explosives, pistols equipped with silencers, double-barreled rifles, false Canadian and U.S. passports, and a large amount of cash. In assessing al-Safadi's capture, Hugo Alfredo Anzorreguy, the director of the Secretariat for State Intelligence (Secretaría de Información del Estado—SIDE), told *O Estado de São Paulo*'s Buenos Aires correspondent that the event had two elements of great significance to continental security: "The first is the existence of cells of terrorists and narcotics traffickers who attempt to infiltrate themselves into some Arab communities," and the second is that "the only way to confront that threat is through regional cooperation."[45]

Although extradited to the United States and sentenced to 18 months in prison, al-Qadi was deported to Canada, where he received a nine-year prison sentence for drug trafficking.

---

[44] Mufid 'Abd-al-Rahim, "Report on Islamic Terrorism in Iguazu Triangle," *Al-Watan al-'Arabi* [Paris], January 9, 1998, 22-24, as translated by FBIS-TOT-98-014, January 15, 1998.

However, al-Safadi escaped from Canada's prisons three times, finally succeeding in escaping from prison in Montreal with the help of Hizballah elements in that area and fleeing to South America with a false passport. Although arrested by Brazilian authorities, he again escaped three times from prison in Brazil before reaching Ciudad del Este.[46]

In 1997 Argentine President Carlos Menem and Brazilian President Fernando Cardoso decided to create a commission charged with developing a security plan for the Triborder Region. Argentina's Minister of Interior Carlos Corach told news media on November 19, 1997, that intelligence reports had alerted the government to a very noticeable increase in the activity of Iranian fundamentalists in the Muslim community in the Triborder Region. Corach explained that Argentine services had established the existence of "sleeper terrorist cells in the region."

In May 1998, Moshen Rabbani, who had served as cultural attaché in the Iranian Embassy in Argentina until December 1997, was detained in Germany. The Argentine government announced that it had "convincing proof" of Iranian involvement in the bombing and expelled seven Iranian diplomats from the country. Rabbani was alleged to have assisted in planning both the 1992 and 1994 bombings along with four Iranian spies who entered the country from Ciudad del Este. According to reports in the Argentine press, Iranian involvement was corroborated by intercepted telephone conversations from the Iranian Embassy and testimony from Ismanian Khosrow, one of the detained Iranians. Since then, however, the investigation has been stalled and none of the suspects have been prosecuted.[47]

On September 2, 1999, Argentine authorities issued an arrest warrant for Imad Fayez Mughniyah in connection with the 1992 embassy bombing. He was later indicted for the AMIA atrocity as well. Investigators said that the indictment was based upon "conclusive evidence" that the bombing had been explicitly ordered by Hizballah, and they determined that handwriting on documents related to the purchase of the truck used in the bombing were those of Hizballah representatives.[48] The truck was bought by a Brazilian known to have contacts with Hizballah

---

[45] H.R., "Paraguai extradita terrorista para Canadá: O `Houdini Árabe' é suspeito de um complô contra a embaixada dos EUA" (Paraguay Extradites Terrorist to Canada: The Houdini Arab is Suspected of a Plot Against the U.S. Embassy), *O Estado de S. Paulo* [São Paulo], January 10, 1998.

[46] Ibid.

[47] Blanca Madani, "New Report Links Syria to 1992 Bombing of Israeli Embassy in Argentina," *Middle East Intelligence Bulletin*, 2, No. 3, March 2000.

[48] "Argentina Issues Arrest Warrant for Senior Hezbollah Leader," *Middle East Intelligence Bulletin*, 1, No. 9, September 1999.

agents in southern Paraguay; it was then driven over the border into Argentina by those who carried out the attack.

On December 22, 1999, the same day that Iran said it was pulling out of its Colombian slaughterhouse project (see Colombia), security officials in Paraguay, Brazil, and Argentina visited people they believed were linked with Hamas and Hizballah. The authorities suspected that terrorist acts were planned in Ciudad del Este, Paraguay; Foz do Iguaçu, Brazil; and Puerto Iguazú, Argentina; according to *ABC Color*. Among the people the authorities visited was a suspected member of Iran's Ministry of Intelligence and Security.[49]

Francis X. Taylor, the Department of State's coordinator for counterterrorism, told Congress on October 10, 2001, that the Triborder Region has "...the longstanding presence of Islamic extremist organizations, primarily Hizballah, and, to a lesser extent, the Sunni extremist groups, such as the Egyptian Islamic Group (Gamaat i-Islami) and Hamas."[50] According to Taylor, the activities of these organizations include fundraising and proselytizing among the zone's Middle Eastern population, as well as document forging, money laundering, contraband smuggling, and weapons and drug trafficking.

Another relatively unknown Islamic extremist group operating in the Triborder Region is al-Muqawamah (the Resistance), which is linked to Lebanon's Hizballah and Iran. *ABC Color* reported in January 2000 that Brazilian and Paraguayan experts were analyzing photographs of Arab extremists taken at the al Mukawama training camp (see Sobhi Mahmoud Fayad), possibly located at a farm in Foz do Iguaçu, Brazil. The men in the photos included several businessmen. They were photographed beside an Iranian flag and a flag from al-Muqawamah. Another photograph is said to show a Hizballah leader reading a letter from Imad Mounigh, presumably wanted Hizballah activist Imad Mughniyah.[51]

Radicalization of Mosques in the Triborder Region

Authorities have suspected that local mosques in the region serve as recruiting centers and collection agencies for Hizballah. Although Argentine security forces have identified Sheik

---

[49]Bill Samii, *Iran Report* [RFE/RL News], December 27, 1999.
[50]Anthony Faiola, "U.S. Terrorist Search Reaches Paraguay; Black Market Border Hub Called Key Finance Center for Middle East Extremists," *Washington Post*, October 13, 2001, A21.
[51] London Bureau Roundup of Terrorism Issues/Developments in the Mideast/Islamic World and the Aegean Derived From Sources Monitored by FBIS, "Latin America: Islamic Fundamentalists in Colombia, Paraguay," FBIS GMP20020109000400, January 10, 2002.

Mounir Fadel, spiritual leader of Ciudad del Este's main mosque, as a senior Hizbullah member, he denies that he is involved in any political activity.

Clarín [Buenos Aires], citing official sources, reported that, by mid-1999, the SIDE was investigating Islamic extremist groups in the Triborder Region that allegedly were operating under the orders of bin Laden.[52] The SIDE investigation resulted from a shared belief that Iran was no longer the only concern in regard to terrorist cells operating in Ciudad del Este (Paraguay) and Foz do Iguaçu (Brazil). That conviction was based on information from the SIDE's own files and from other intelligence services, which reported that bin Laden had gained ground in the Triborder Region as a result of Iran's partial withdrawal from the important Arab community in the area, thanks to Iranian President Mohamed Khatami.[53]

Using hidden cameras carried by agents infiltrating the groups, or cameras installed at locations near the Mosques, SIDE agents filmed meetings of the Shi'ite and minority Sunni groups who were part of the sizeable Moslem population in the Triborder Region. The SIDE used these films to make a map of all the mosques in Foz do Iguaçu and Ciudad del Este, identifying each mosque and matching it up with the Moslem group that it supported in the Middle East conflict. The SIDE agents also taped the group's telephone calls to the Middle East.[54]

The SIDE had also reportedly detected a significant development concerning the traditionally sectarian nature of Muslim terrorist groups in the Triborder Region.[55] Until about 1999, pro-Iranian Shiite extremists organizations, such as the Islamic Jihad or the Lebanese Hizballah faction—to which the bombing of the Argentine-Israeli Mutual Association (AMIA) is

---

[52] "Bin Laden's Followers in Triborder Area Probed," FBIS, WA1907180899, July 19, 1999, translating Daniel Santoro, *Clarín* [Buenos Aires; an Independent, tabloid-format daily; highest-circulation newspaper, Internet version], July 18, 1999.

[53] Ibid.

[54] "Argentine Intelligence Services' 1999 Report on Usamah Bin-Ladin's Agents in Triborder Area Viewed," FBIS LAP20010916000021, September 16, 2001, translating Daniel Santoro, *Clarín*, September 16, 2001, 8-9.

[55] Tânia Monteiro, DPA, EFE, and France Presse, "Tríplice fronteira tinha agentes sauditas, diz "Clarín" [TriBorder has Saudi agents, *Clarín* says], Estadao Website, September 17, 2001.

attributed—normally worked separately from the pro-Saudi, orthodox Sunnites and followed instructions from Teheran. By mid-1999, however, SIDE's sources were saying that: "There is currently no operational difference between the Sunnites and the Shiites" in the Triborder Region, from where the detonators and passports used in the attack on the AMIA Jewish cultural center are thought to have entered the country. In the Triborder Region, according to the SIDE's sources, "…the Sunnite organization maintains various contacts with elements suspected of being Hizballah sympathizers or affiliates."[56] According to *Clarín*, the SIDE's reports were received with skepticism by the CIA and Israel's Mossad, however.

According to official sources consulted by *Clarín*, the report further reads: "Minority groups respond to bin Laden as some of the influences of the Iranians and Hizballah fade. They collect funds, indoctrinate others, take in fugitives, and offer basic military training, such as how to build homemade bombs, but they have not set up any training camps."[57] Since the SIDE investigation began, however, the top Hizballah and al Qaeda agents reportedly have left Ciudad del Este and Foz do Iguaçu for more isolated locations on the border between Bolivia and Brazil, or have gone directly back to the Middle East.[58]

Concern about factional infighting among moderate and radical Hizballah adherents in the Triborder Region was renewed when Sheikh Akram Ahmad Barakat, brother of Assad Ahmad Barakat (see profile below), the alleged Hizballah military chief in the Triborder Region, interviewed Said Mohammad Fahs, leader of the Ciudad del Este Islamic Education Center and the local Shia mosque.[59] Contending that Fahs was not teaching correctly, Akram Barakat had opened a new Islamic Center, which was supposedly connected with Hizballah. Subsequently, Akram Barakat was hiding in Brazil to avoid arrest by Paraguayan anti-terror forces operating near Ciudad del Este. *ABC Color* reported that, "Regional intelligence sources have identified Sheikh Akram Ahmad Barakat, who resides in Iran, as a kind of roving Iranian ambassador for Latin America." According to London's *Al-Sharq al-Awsat*, Fals, who was shot and wounded by unidentified gunmen in November 1999, subsequently claimed that his opponents, having failed

---

[56] "Bin Laden's Followers in Triborder Area Probed," FBIS, WA1907180899, July 19, 1999, translating Daniel Santoro, *Clarín* (Internet version), July 18, 1999.

[57] "Argentine Intelligence Services' 1999 Report on Usamah Bin-Ladin's Agents in Triborder Area Viewed," FBIS LAP20010916000021, September 16, 2001, translating Daniel Santoro, *Clarín*, September 16, 2001, 8-9.

[58] Ibid.

[59] Comp. A. William Samii, "Competition Among South American Hizballah Resumes," *Iran Report* [RFE/RL], July 17, 2000, 3, No. 27, citing *ABC Color*, July 12, 2000.

to assassinate him, were trying to blackmail him.[60] Fahs represents the wing with a "conciliatory attitude with Western society," whereas the opposing "radical wing" of Hizballah is led by Bilal Mohsen Wehbi, who is supposedly "pro-Iranian."[61]

There have been other indications of factional infighting among the Islamic community in Ciudad del Este and possible terrorist activity. For example, according to Brazilian press reports, Gueddan Abdel Fatah, 27, a Moroccan student arrested in early September 2001 in Brazil on charges of assaulting a taxi in São Paulo, contacted an attorney visiting his prison on September 5, asking her to "urgently" deliver a letter to Brazilian, U.S., and Israeli authorities. He said that he wanted to warn them about an impending attack with "two explosions" that could take place in the United States. Later, Fatah told authorities he had learned about the impending attack at a mosque in Foz do Iguaçu, on the Brazilian border with Ciudad del Este.

Investigations into terrorist connections in the Triborder Region prompted Hizballah leaders in the area to issue a fatwa authorizing the use of physical violence against traitors or enemies of the holy war. According to intelligence agents cited by *Última Hora*, the fatwa was issued on November 2, 2001, during a funeral service at a mosque.[62]

The Triborder Region: A Funding Source for Islamic Fundamentalist Terrorism?

Brazilian authorities have estimated that more than $6 billion a year in illegal funds is laundered in the Triborder Region. Argentina's Ramon Mestre, director of the Permanent Work Group (Grupo de Trabajo Permanente—GTP), founded to establish a coordinated common policy against terrorism in the countries that make up Mercosur, admitted in early December 2001 that the Triborder Region had given "logistical support to terrorist organizations by providing money to groups that operate in other parts of the world." He said that activities such as the illegal traffic of immigrants and drug trafficking in the region "are elements that are in some way linked to terrorism...."[63] An estimated 1.5 tons of cocaine per month are exported. Every evening, a dozen armored trucks loaded with laundered money leave Ciudad del Este for Foz do Iguaçu, the Brazilian town on the opposite side of the border.

---

[60] *Iran Report* [RFE/RL], January 10, 2000.
[61] "Competition Among South American Hizballah," RFE/RL, February 6, 2002, translating ABC Color, January 5, 2002; URL: http://www.rferl.org/iran-report/2000/01/2-100100.html
[62] "FBIS Report: Media on Efforts to Combat Terrorist Financial Activity in Triborder Area," LAP20011210000096, December 10, 2001, translating Asunción's *Útima Hora*, November 5, 2001.

According to Blanca Madani, co-president of the World Amazigh Action Coalition (WAAC), Hizballah—in addition to the estimated $60 to $100 million per year that it receives from Iran—has also relied extensively on funding from the Shi'ite Lebanese Diaspora in West Africa, the United States, and most importantly the Triborder Region of Argentina, Brazil, and Paraguay.[64] In early January 1998, the Brazilian newspaper *Estado de São Paulo* cited Argentine reporter Hernán López Accago [name as transliterated], who had just published a book on drug and arms smuggling in the Triborder Region, as saying that many businessmen in the region pay what amounts to a war tax to the armed Arab groups in the region.[65] This money is used in financing military operations in various parts of the world.

During the 1999-2001 period, Islamic extremist groups received at least $50 million from Arab residents in the area of Foz do Iguaçu, Paraná State, through Paraguayan financial institutions, such as banks and exchange houses. The U.S. and Paraguayan governments obtained evidence that the Lebanese Hizballah group and the Palestinian Hamas group received funds from Arab residents of Foz do Iguaçu. Paraguayan Interior Minister Julio César Fanego was quoted as saying: "We verified the remittance of money [to Arab extremist groups]. I am almost sure that there are citizens linked to the Hizballah in the Triborder Region. . . .The exact figure will probably be something between $50 and $500 million." The minister explained that most of the money remittance operations included very small amounts of money, between $500 and $2,000.[66] The joint Paraguayan-U.S.

---

[63] *El País* [Montevideo], December 1, 2001, translated in "Uruguay Press Highlights," FBIS LAP20011203000074, December 3, 2001.

[64] Blanca Madani, "Hezbollah's Global Finance Network: The Triple Frontier," *Middle East Intelligence Bulletin* [a monthly publication of the United States Committee for a Free Lebanon], 4, No. 1, January 2002.

[65] "Brazil: Report on Islamic Terrorism in Iguazu Triangle," *al-Watan al-'Arabi* [Paris], January 9, 1998, 22-24, as cited by *Estado de São Paulo*.

[66] Roberto Cosso, "Extremistas receberam US$50 mi de Foz do Iguaçu" (Extremists Received US$50 million from Foz do Iguaçu), *Folha de S. Paulo*, December 3, 2001.

investigation focused on 45 names listed by Paraguay's Secretariat for the Prevention of Money Laundering as individuals who carried out money remittance operations of more than $100,000 and from four individuals listed by U.S. authorities: Assad Ahmad Barakat and three of his employees—Sobhi Mahmoud Fayad, Mazen Ali Saleh, and Saleh or Salhed Mahmoud Fayad (Sobhi's brother).[67]

Brazilian security agencies claimed that the financial aid offered in 2000 by groups in the Triborder Region to Islamic and Middle Eastern terrorist organizations, such as Hizballah, Hamas, and the Islamic Jihad, totaled $261 million. The report noted the strengthening influence of organized crime networks in the triangle comprising various nationalities—Colombians, Brazilians, Chinese, Lebanese, Nigerians, Russians, Ghanaians, and individuals from the Ivory Coast. These groups are active in Paraguay and along the drug trafficking route from Colombia to the United States and Europe. The report noted that most of these clandestine operations take place in Ciudad del Este, considered a regional center for drug trafficking and arms smuggling. The transactions mostly involve bartering drugs for weapons from Colombian armed rebel groups.[68]

The Brazilian figure of $261 million of financial aid provided to terrorist groups in 2000 alone makes a report released by the Bolivian government in November 2001 seem like an underestimate. According to the Bolivian report, more than $250 million of suspected drug money was transferred from Brazil to a Lebanese bank, via Bolivia, during the previous seven years.[69] Ramiro Rivas Montealegre, the director of Bolivia's Financial Unit, explained that there are "indications of a link between arms traffickers, drug traffickers and international terrorists." Authorities in Brazil were investigating 10 Lebanese citizens living there who are allegedly involved in money laundering. On October 2, 2001, Lebanese-born Mazen Ali Saleh and Saleh or Salhed Mahmoud Fayad (Sobhi Mahmoud Fayad's brother), both in their 20s, were arrested in Ciudad del Este, in possession of documents indicating regular remittances of between $25,000

---

[67] Ibid.

[68] Riyadh Alam-al-Din, "Washington Begins the War on Hizballah in the Border Triangle," *Al-Watan al-Arabi* [Paris], December 21, 2001, 18-19, as translated by FBIS, GMP20011221000179, "Report Says US Antiterror Campaign To Target Hizballah Network in S. America."

[69] "Government Keeps Watchful Eye on Paraguay's Arab Community," October 13, 2001, EFE News Services, FBIS Rec. No. OEF2C4F9D99922F0.

and $50,000 to suspected Muslim radicals. They were both linked to Assad Ahmad Barakat, whom investigators suspect of being the chief Southern Cone fund-raiser for Hizballah.[70]

In early December 2001, *ABC Color* reported that Basilisa Vázquez Román, a prosecutor in Ciudad del Este, for the previous two months had been investigating a $100 million transfer from Ciudad del Este to Lebanon. According to information provided to the Brazilian media by Vázquez Román, 10 Lebanese citizens who own businesses in Ciudad del Este but live in Foz do Iguaçu, Brazil, sent the money through banks in Miami and New York to Lebanese banks. According to the investigation, the deposits were made in Ciudad del Este branches of Citibank and Chinatrust. Each Lebanese sent approximately $6 to $10 million. Although Vázquez Román had not determined the destination of the money, he was continuing the investigation.[71]

Suspected al Qaeda Cells in the Triborder Region

In an interview with Brazil's *O Globo* newspaper in September 2001, Jude Walter Fanganiello Maierovitch, former National Drug Enforcement secretary and one of the leading Latin American experts on money laundering and the activities of international mafias, said that al Qaeda is establishing a base near Ciudad del Este, in an Arab community of 30,000 people.[72] Maierovitch explained that bin Laden wants to establish a presence in the Triborder Region because al Qaeda's terrorist activities are linked with the trafficking of arms, drugs, and uranium, as well as money laundering, in association with the Russian and Chinese mafias. Operating behind religious entities, bin Laden's goal would be to train terrorists and provide a hiding place for Islamic fugitives, according to Maierovitch. He added that bin Laden is winning over members of the Hizballah group that allegedly bombed the Jewish beneficent association in Buenos Aires in 1994. He also confirmed that the Russian and Chinese mafias are increasingly present in Paraguay, and are now associated with bin Laden.

---

[70] "Government Keeps Watchful Eye on Paraguay's Arab Community," October 13, 2001, EFE News Services, FBIS Rec. No. OEF2C4F9D99922F0.

[71] *ABC Color*, December 5, 2001, as translated by FBIS LAP20011210000096, "FBIS Report: Media on Efforts to Combat Terrorist Financial Activity in Triborder Area," December 10, 2001.

[72] "Brazil's Former Drug Czar: Bin-Ladin Establishing Al-Qa'idah Cell on Triborder," translating Germano Oliveira, *O Globo*, September 19, 2001: Document ID: LAP200109119000051.

Rio de Janeiro's *O Globo* reported in late October 2001 that the FBI, in close collaboration with the CIA, had discovered evidence that al Qaeda is making the Triborder Region between Brazil, Paraguay, and Argentina its main center of operations in Latin America. The area, described by U.S. authorities as a "no-man's-land," is allegedly a logistics headquarters, the base for two specific depots. One depot is financial, centralizing the collections of contributions to the Islamic cause. The other is that of drug trafficking, and it supposedly has a direct connection with the Revolutionary Armed Forces of Colombia (FARC) (also see Colombia). As of late October 2001, Brazil's Justice Minister José Gregori lacked knowledge of any "conclusive information" on al Qaeda cells in Brazil, according to *O Globo*. "We have a Federal Police task force in the region and a joint effort with the governments of the other countries, and to date nothing conclusive has been found," he told the newspaper. "This is not the first time that news reports of this type have appeared, which end up hurting Foz do Iguaçu, which has already had a 40 percent drop in tourist traffic."[73] The reluctance of Brazilian government officials to acknowledge the country's use as a base for an Islamic terrorism support network may also have been predicated on fears that the disclosure of activities of extremist groups on its territory would permit the United States to demand Brazil's more active involvement in the "war against terrorism."

On October 18, 2001, Argentina's foreign ministry disclosed that its embassy in Riyadh, Saudi Arabia, had received telephone calls—purportedly from al Qaeda—on September 20, 23, and 24, 2000, warning that an attack on a U.S. target was planned for September 26, 2000 (the U.S. naval destroyer *USS Cole* was hit by suicide bombers in Aden harbor on October 12, 2000, killing 17 American service personnel). The embassy also received a call on October 26, 2000, claiming responsibility for an unspecified 'explosion' in Argentina. Argentine judicial sources

---

[73] José Meirelles Passos, "The Shadow of Bin Ladin in Latin America," *O Globo* (Internet Version-WWW), October 29, 2001, as translated by FBIS LAP20011029000036, "Brazil: Daily Notes US Views Triborder as Al-Qa'idah Center for L.A.," October 29, 2001.

believe that the callers to the Riyadh embassy were referring to the July 18, 1994, attack on the AMIA community center.[74]

In early February 2002, Paraguayan and foreign security forces as well as Brazilian, Argentine, Israeli, and U.S. agents were searching the Triborder Region, especially Ciudad del Este and Foz do Iguaçu, for five Afghan citizens who allegedly belong to the Taliban and are linked to al Qaeda, either as supporters or members.[75] Each of the individuals allegedly was carrying three or four sets of different identity documents.

Clandestine Telephone Exchanges Used by Extremists

Before the September 11 attacks in the United States, Brazilian investigators were suspicious of what was thought to be merely illegal schemes to reduce the price of telephone calls. After September 11, however, suspicions shifted to possible terrorist links because the illegal calls went to countries like Afghanistan, Pakistan, and Lebanon. Concerned about what it considered to be the action of Islamic extremist cells in the Triborder Region, a team from the Brazilian Federal Police (Policia Federal—PF) Intelligence Coordination (CI) started to operate secretly in the region. The following month, the PF discovered various clandestine telephone exchanges suspected of links with Islamic extremism.[76]

Twelve of the illegal telephone exchanges were discovered in Brazil. One of the exchanges in Taguatinga, Federal District, registered more than 1,000 calls to the Middle East on the occasion of the September 11, 2001, terrorist attacks. A telecommunications device capable of communicating worldwide was found at a plantation in Rio Branco, Acre State. At an exchange operated in Campo Grande, Mato Grosso do Sul State, Rubens Nunes Garcia and Lebanese nationals Jamil Alkayal, 24, and his father, Ghassan Jamil, 47, a resident of Paraguay, made connections with Afghanistan, Lebanon, Pakistan, and Angola. They also operated an

---

[74] "Al-Qaeda and Argentina," *Jane's Intelligence Digest*, October 26, 2001.
[75] *ABC Color* web site, February 5, 2002, as cited by "International Security Forces Search for Five Afghan fugitives in Paraguay," BBC Monitoring Service [UK], February 5, 2002.

exchange in São Paulo. The trio was arrested under suspicion of belonging to a Taliban network.[77] Nunes Garcia was the leader of the group, which also included two women. At their residence, police found Arabic texts, nondecipherable codes, and a notebook with notations of various telephone numbers and copies of documents.[78]

The largest center of clandestine connections in the country, in Maringá, Paraná State, had five exchanges with 57 lines. It registered more than 600 calls to Asian and Middle Eastern countries. In Foz do Iguaçu, police arrested Lebanese Muhamed Hassan Atwi and the Brazilian Paulo César Caramori. In the apartment used by the two men, police found a computer and false passports. In addition to the illegal telephone services in Paraná, Atwi was suspected of operating another in Rio de Janeiro.[79] In Cascavel, police discovered an unpaid telephone bill of R$95,000 for calls made to Afghanistan in the name of José Fátima Carnietto.

Telephone exchanges equipped with PABX for connecting among telephone networks were used by suspected Islamic extremists for establishing secure communication between two parties abroad, almost always based in countries named "high risk" for terrorists. Telecommunications experts concluded that the real reason for the Brazilian connection was to evade eavesdropping on telephone conversations by spy satellites. Calls from Saudi Arabia to Brazil, or from Brazil to Pakistan, for example, could be made without raising suspicions.

One of the most active networks was in Maringá, in Paraná State. The exchanges connected 57 lines. One of the operators of the equipment, Ederaldo Félix dos Santos, 33, told *O Globo's* Época that he was contracted by Lebanese businessman Afif Adib Eid when Eid was living in Foz do Iguaçu in 1999-2000.[80] Época also interviewed Afif Adib Eid at his house in Foz do Iguaçu in October 2001. Eid, 33, owns an electronic products store in Ciudad del Este, in Paraguay. He migrated from Lebanon to Brazil in 1989. Eid claimed that his telephone scheme had nothing to do with terrorism, but served only as a means to communicate with his family in Beirut.

---

[76] Expedito Filho and Sílvio Ferreira, with Patrícia Cerqueira, "Rede de clandestinidade" (Clandestine Network), OnlineÉpoca Editora Globo], No. 179, October 22, 2001.

[77] João Naves de Oliveira, "Central telefônica leva três à prisão em MS" (Telephone Exchange Takes Three to Prison in MS), Estado.com.br, October 12, 2001.

[78] "Árabes teriam financiado centrais telefônicas piratas no PR" (Arabs Had Financed Pirated Telephone Exchanges in PR), Estadao.com.br, terra.com.br, October 11, 2001.

[79] Ibid.

[80] "O terror por aqui" (The terror at Home), OnLine Epoca, O Globo.com, No. 179, October 22, 2001.

Alleged Operatives of Islamic Fundamentalist Groups in the Triborder Region

Barakat, Assad Ahmad Mohamad (Hizballah)

Assad Mohamed Barakat is generally identified as the Hizballah military chief in the Triborder Region. He is also believed to be heavily involved in Hazballah funding operations in the region. Following the September 11, 2001, terrorist attacks in the United States, an international arrest warrant was issued for his arrest. According to an article in Spain's daily *El País*, Barakat is suspected of being a "high-ranking Hizballah military chief" who sends large amounts of money to the Middle East.[81]

Assad Barakat left civil-war-torn Lebanon at age 17 and emigrated to Paraguay with his father, a taxi driver. After a few years as a street peddler, he opened a closet-sized Apollo Import-Export stall in the crowded and shabby Page gallery in Ciudad del Este. His four brothers and a sister in Lebanon later emigrated to Paraguay to join him. According to his Paraguayan passport, Barakat was last in the United States in April 2000, but his visa was revoked after his name appeared on the U.S. Department of State's list of "suspected terrorists."

On September 12, 2001, a Paraguayan SWAT team raided Barakat's stall in the Page shopping center, but Barakat, 34, was away on business and escaped arrest. The police confiscated more than 60 hours of videotapes and CD-ROMs. The latter show military marches and attacks with explosives in various parts of the world, as well as speeches by Hassan Nasrahhal, the main leader of the Hizballah.[82] In an AP interview, Barakat explained that the seized videos were sent six years earlier by relatives in Lebanon, but that "we don't need them any more because we get our information from Al-Manar," the Hizballah satellite channel

---

[81] Héctor Rojas and Pablo Vergara, *La Tercera de la Hora* [Santiago; a conservative, pro-business, top-circulation daily, Internet Version-WWW], November 8, 2001, as translated in "Chilean Police Examine Link to Alleged Triborder Hizballah Financial Network," FBIS, LAP20011108000085, November 8, 2001.

[82] José Maschio, "Paraguayan Court Evidence Cited on Hizballah Link at Triborder," *Folha de São Paulo* [Internet Version-WWW], November 26, 2001, as translated by FBIS LAP20011126000074.

recently made available in the Triborder Region.[83] The confiscated material also included professional training courses for suicide bombers. Paraguayan prosecutor Carlos Cálcena told *Folha* that "Barakat and his companions were recruiting and used these speeches as propaganda."

According to the *Washington Post*, citing Paraguayan officers, the SWAT team also seized boxes containing financial statements totaling $250,000 in monthly transfers to the Middle East and descriptions of at least 30 recent attacks in Israel and the Israeli-occupied territories.[84] According to Cálcena, Paraguay's Terrorism Prevention and Investigations Department found that Barakat and Salah sent money to international terrorist bank accounts in various countries, specifically $505,200 to Canada, Chile (see Chile, below), and the United States (New York), and banks drafts of $524,000 to Lebanon. Paraguayan Police found a letter from the Hizballah commander congratulating Barakat for financing activities in the Middle East.[85]

Argentine police have described the Page shopping center as the regional command post for Hizballah. According to the *Wall Street Journal*, Argentine police have a thick dossier on Barakat that includes photographs showing him and a brother at a Brazilian mosque that the police described as a central Hizballah meeting place. Argentine police also claimed that Barakat was involved in contributing $60 million in counterfeit U.S. dollars printed in Colombia. Argentine law enforcement officials reportedly believe that Barakat has links to Hizballah cells in Buenos Aires, and that he helped to carry out the 1994 bombing of the Jewish community center. Nevertheless, Barakat has not been indicted in Argentina because of a lack of evidence.

Arrested by Paraguayan Police in October 2001, Barakat escaped from prison and fled to Brazil, where, as a Brazilian citizen, he was not considered to be a security threat. In early January 2002, Barakat, despite three arrest warrants filed against him with Interpol, remained free in the Brazilian city of Curitiba. Barakat apparently resides in either Foz do Iguaçu or Curitiba with his Brazilian wife and three sons.

---

[83] Stan Lehman, "Wanted by Paraguay, Hezbollah Supporter Is Free in Brazilian Town Across the Border," AP, December 12, 2001.
[84] Anthony Faiola, "U.S. Terrorist Search Reaches Paraguay; Black Market Border Hub Called Key Finance Center for Middle East Extremists," *Washington Post*, October 13, 2001, A21.
[85] Ricardo Galhardo Enviado, "Paraguai pede a prisão de libanês no Brasil" (Paraguay Sentences a Lebanese in Brazil to Prison), *O Globo*, November 6, 2001.

According to Brazilian military intelligence sources cited by *O Estado de São Paulo*, Barakat's business and Hizballah partner, Salman Reda, who fled on the same day as Barakat, was charged in Argentina with transporting explosives used against the Israeli Embassy. In late November 2001, Barakat's employees in the Apollo shop—Sobhi Mahmoud Fayad, Mazen Ali Saleh, and Saleh or Salhed Mahmoud Fayad (Sobhi's brother)—were under arrest in Asunción, charged with forming a gang, aiding and abetting a crime, tax evasion, and product piracy.

According to *Folha de São Paulo*, a Federal Police (PF) intelligence report sent by Brazil to Paraguayan authorities between late 1999 and early 2000 reportedly mentions three Hizballah leaders with whom Barakat allegedly met during trips to Lebanon that were annual at minimum. The PF Register of Foreigners affirms that Barakat, the businessman, "is thought to be one of the Hizballah leaders in the region, where he arrived in 1987." As of 2002, the PF reportedly had not found any evidence linking the funds that Barakat allegedly sent to the Middle East with terrorist groups. Nevertheless, there appears to be substantial evidence that Barakat is linked to Hizballah.

Asunción's *Última Hora* reported in early December 2001 that the intelligence services, which were collecting information on the activities of Lebanese citizens living in the Triborder Region, had found more evidence on how Assad Barakat collected money for Hizballah. According to the evidence, Barakat used blackmail and even death threats to force other Lebanese citizens to contribute to the Muslim fundamentalist group. Prosecutor Carlos Cálcena discovered that Barakat used private contracts to get loans and that he was only identified as NN in the contracts.[86]

---

[86] "Barakat Resorted to Blackmail To Get Money," *Última Hora* (Asunción, an independent, centrist daily), December 6, 2001, as translated by FBIS Report: Media on Efforts to Combat Terrorist Financial Activity in Triborder Area," LAP20011210000096, December 10, 2001.

Fayad, Sobhi Mahmoud (Hizballah)

Sobhi Mahmoud Fayad, who claims to be a Lebanese businessman but is widely reported to be a key Hizballah operative, was arrested on November 8, 2001, in the center of Ciudad del Este, as he fled from the Page Shopping Gallery after noticing that the police were approaching to arrest him.[87] Fayad was arrested on the orders of Prosecutor Carlos Arregui on charges of being an alleged member of an organization that remits funds to the Islamic Middle East armed struggle. Documents that were found at the Apollo shop owned by Assad Barakat allegedly incriminate Sobhi Fayad. On the basis of the documents, it was alleged that Sobhi Fayad, who has not paid taxes since 1992, was sending large sums of money to banks in Lebanon almost daily. Sobhi Fayad was arrested reportedly because of his alleged ties with Assad Ahmad Barakat, who is at large and who has been alleged to be the head of the Hizballah military wing.

In early January 2002, Paraguayan police explained that Sobhi Mahmoud Fayad was being held for tax evasion, money laundering, and "threatening the people's coexistence." He remained under arrest in the Police Special Operations Force unit in Asunción together with his brother Salhed Fayad.

The Paraguayan National Police's Antiterrorism Department (DAT) reportedly believes that Sobhi Mahmoud Fayad, along with Assad Barakat and fugitive Ali Hassan Abdallah, are the coordinators of a Hizballah financial network in the Triborder Region. In addition, Fayad is a brother of an important Hizballah member in Lebanon. The DAT reportedly regards Sobhi Mahmoud Fayad as one of the main Hizballah chiefs assigned to the Triborder Region.[88] Police found in his possession documents for funds sent to Canada and Lebanon. Fayad's influence within the Lebanese community in the Triborder Region was emphasized by reports that he was seen in the company of the new Lebanese

---

[87] *ABC Color* Web site, November 9, 2001, as cited by "Paraguay: Lebanese Man with Alleged Hezbollah Links Arrested in Ciudad del Este," BBC Monitoring, November 9, 2001.

[88] Libanês preso no Paraguai é "peso pesado" do Hezbollah, diz polícia" (Lebanese Imprisoned in Paraguay Is a Hizballah Heavyweight, Police Say), estadao.com.br [Website of *O Estado de São Paulo*], November 9, 2001.

ambassador in Paraguay, Hicham Hamdam, who presented his credential in Asunción in October 2001, on various occasions when the diplomat attended local activities.

A letter that Sobhi Mahmoud Fayad received from Lebanon allegedly proves that in 2000 alone he sent more than $3.5 million to the "Martyr" Social Beneficent Organization, which is linked to the Hizballah and which looks after children whose parents died at the service of the Hizballah and who are considered martyrs. The letter, which is written in Arabic, was confiscated from Barakat's store and translated. It begins with the title: "To all those who complied with the call of the envoy of God." It states: "We are placing in your hands the results of your direct cooperation for the maintenance of the orphans and martyrs throughout 2000. The total payment during 2000 amounted to $3,535,149."[89]

In January 2002, Paraguay's antiterrorist group monitoring the activities of alleged Arab terrorists in the Triborder Region detected an Al Mukawama operations center in the area of Tres Lagoas, Foz do Iguaçu.[90] Al Mukawama is the pro-Iran wing of the Hizballah. According to the investigators' report to court authorities, alleged Hizballah fundamentalist groups are indoctrinated, recruited, and trained in the operations center. The investigators confirmed the presence of Sobhi Mahmoud Fayad at the Al Mukawama operations center. According to Interior Ministry sources, he appears in one of the surveillance photos chatting with Iman Tareb Khasraji (on left in photo) in early November 2001.

Paraguayan authorities had arrested Mahmoud Fayad even earlier, in 1998, while he was observing the U.S. Embassy in Asunción, either before or after requesting an appointment in the facility. However, he was later released after cooperating with authorities.[91] He was again arrested in front of the U.S. Embassy in Asunción in October 1999, after having requested a visa. On that occasion, he was questioned on the basis of the suspicions of U.S. officials, but he was later released for lack of evidence against him. When he was released in 1999, Fayad said that he had no ties with extremists and that he was only a businessman.

---

[89] Roberto Cosso, "Extremistas receberam US$50 mi de Foz do Iguaçu" (Extremists Received US$50 million from Foz do Iguaçu), *Folha de S. Paulo*, December 3, 2001.
[90] *ABC Color* [Internet Version-WWW], January 16, 2002, as translated by FBIS LAP20020116000091, "Paraguay: Court Investigates Hizballah Base Photos."
[91] "Libanês preso no Paraguai," op cit.

Mehri, Ali Khalil (Hizballah)

The relationship between the Triborder underworld and Middle East terrorism became clearer in February 2000, when Paraguayan authorities arrested Ali Khalil Mehri, 32, a newly naturalized Paraguayan citizen born in Lebanon, who was living in Ciudad del Este. Mehri was charged with selling millions of dollars of counterfeit software and funneling the proceeds to Hizballah. Police searched his home and confiscated videos and CDs of known suicide bombers rallying others to their cause. According to the police, a CD confiscated from his store in the Triple Frontier contained images of "terrorist propaganda of the extremist group Al-Muqawama," which belongs to Hizballah. Other documents seized during the raid included fundraising forms for a group in the Middle East named Al-Shahid, ostensibly dedicated to "the protection of families of martyrs and prisoners," as well as documents of money transfers to Canada, Chile, Lebanon, and the United States of more than $700,000.[92] British intelligence subsequently identified Mehri as a potential al Qaeda financier, according to the *Washington Post*. Apparently aided by his large campaign contributions to powerful members of Paraguay's ruling Colorado Party, Mehri escaped from prison in June 2000 and fled to Syria. One of Khalil Mehri's main defenders and protectors was Paraguay's Deputy Angel Ramón Barchini. According to *ABC Color*, the U.S. Embassy cancelled the visa issued to Deputy Barchini to enter the United States because of his alleged links with suspicious Arab extremists.[93]

Mukhlis, El Said Hassan Ali Mohamed (Al-Gama'a al-Islamiyya)

Argentina's SIDE has investigated the Egyptian Al-Sa'id Ali Hasan Mukhlis (also spelled Mokhles), 31, who has been identified as having contacts with a group of bin Laden militants in the Triborder Region. Mukhlis, an Egyptian who had trained in Afghanistan and was a member of the Islamic fundamentalist group Al-Gama'a al-Islamiyya, was suspected of participating in the massacre of 62 tourists at Luxor, Egypt in 1997. A native of the coastal city of Port Said, Mukhlis left Egypt in the early 1990s, fearing random arrests of Al-Gama'a members.

---

[92] "Comandos terroristas se refugian en la triple frontera" (Terrorist "Commandos" Hide in the Triborder Region), *El País* [Colombia], November 9, 2001.
[93] *ABC Color*, November 5, 2001, as translated in FBIS, LAP20011105000019, "Barchini's Calls Under Scrutiny, New Antiterrorist Officials," November 5, 2001.

Argentine security suspected that the detonators used in the 1994 AMIA attack were secured in the Triborder Region and linked Mukhlis to that operation. Argentine security believed that Mukhlis established terrorist cells in Foz de Iguaçú to raise funds, to manufacture counterfeit documents, and to maintain contact with Hamas and Hizbullah sympathizers. After living with his family in Foz do Iguaçu in 1998, Mukhlis was arrested at a border control station in El Chuy, Uruguay, on the Brazilian-Uruguayan border on January 26, 1999, as he tried to leave Brazil using a fake Malaysian passport. Contacted by border-control authorities, the CIA reportedly requested that he be detained on charges of having participated in the Luxor terrorist attack. At the time of his arrest, Mukhlis was allegedly en route to Europe for a meeting with another al Qaeda terrorist.

Egypt immediately began a lengthy legal struggle to extradite Mukhlis. In mid-1999 Egypt demanded that Uruguay extradite Mukhlis on the accusation in absentia of having participated in the 1998 bombing attack on more than 60 U.S. and European tourists in the Egyptian city of Luxor.

Mukhlis' wife, Sahar (Sarrah) Mohamed Hassam Abud Hamanra, was arrested along with her husband in 1999 but immediately released. At the time of her arrest in Uruguay, Hamanra produced Brazilian documentation that the PF declared false. She had already been under investigation by the PF for one month. She is on the list of 100 people that the FBI wanted to interview after September 11. Just hours after the hijacked planes crashed into the World Trade Center and the Pentagon, the FBI reportedly requested South American security services to intensify efforts to locate Muhklis' wife, according to the Bogotá weekly magazine, *Cambio*. Law enforcement sources were quoted in the report as saying that Hamanra could be the contact between al Qaeda and the Arab community in the Triborder Region.[94] The FBI reportedly traced several telephone calls between the United States and at least one of the Triborder Region cities immediately following the September 11, 2001, terrorist attacks.

---

[94] Martin Arostegui, "Search for Bin Laden links looks south," www.autentico.org [UPI via COMTEX], October 12, 2001.

According to official sources, citing the SIDE, Mukhlis received military training in Afghanistan from Al-Jama'at al-Islamiyah in the 1980s. He was later sent to Foz do Iguaçu by bin Laden. In that Brazilian city, Mukhlis allegedly "formed terrorist cells to collect funds for the Middle East and to conduct logistical support activities, such as forging passports or other documents. That false documentation was meant for activists in the Islamic Jihad." Furthermore, officials asserted that, "he had a mission to make contact with Hamas and Hizballah sympathizers" in Ciudad del Este, Foz do Iguaçu, and São Paulo. Despite local intelligence reports that Mukhlis might be linked to bin Laden, concrete evidence seems to be lacking.

In a ruling made public on October 5, 2001, an Uruguayan appeals court approved the extradition of Mukhlis, conditioning its approval on commitments from Egypt to not apply the death penalty, to respect due process, and to not try him on the charge of falsification of documents for which he was already convicted in Uruguay. However, an appeal of the ruling to the Supreme Court was expected to take another 12 months. According to a report published on October 5, 2001, in the Uruguayan daily *El Observador*, the appeals court indicated that Mukhlis "was trained in Afghan camps commanded by Saudi terrorist Osama bin Laden, accused of leading the September 11 attacks in the U.S."[95]

Yassine, Salah Abdul Karim (Hamas)

On November 28, 2000, Paraguayan authorities arrested Salah Abdul Karim Yassine, a Palestinian who had entered the country using false documents.[96] He was captured on an estate in the city of Encarnación, on the border with Brazil. He claimed to be a Colombian and produced a passport that had expired in 1997 and contained the name of Jaime Yassine Uribe.[97] Paraguayan authorities accused him of plotting to bomb the U.S. and Israeli embassies in Asunción. According to the *Washington Post*, he was allegedly securing $100,000 in financing while living in

---

[95] *El Nuevo Herald* [Miami], October 6, 2001, from AFP; *New York Times*, November 27, 2001.
[96] *Patterns of Global Terrorism, 2000*, Office of the Coordinator for Counterterrorism, April 30, 2001.
[97] Pedro Doria, "Terrorismo aqui no lado" (Terrorism Here Next Door), www.no.com.br, November 30, 2000.

Ciudad del Este. The FBI, aided by the Mossad, determined that he has Colombian nationality under the name of Jaime Yassin Urabi. He lived in Colombia between 1996 and 1999 and made trips throughout South America. He is believed to be an explosives expert and to have sent a fax to the Israeli Embassy in Asunción threatening it in the name of Hamas.[98] He was sentenced to a four-year prison term on charges of possessing false documents and entering the country illegally.

ISLAMIC FUNDAMENTALIST ACTIVITIES ELSEWHERE IN LATIN AMERICA

Chile

Chile has become the fastest-growing hub in South America after Brazil for international narcotics transshipments and money-laundering enterprises.[99] This fact may help to explain why Islamic money launderers are attracted to the northern Chilean city of Iquique. As pressure from security authorities has increased in the Triborder Region, a number of Islamic militants reportedly have moved to Iquique.

On November 8, 2001, the Chilean Government confirmed that it was investigating an alleged Arab financial network with terrorist links that may be engaging in money laundering in the north of the country.[100] More specifically, Chilean authorities were investigating business ventures in Iquique of Assad Ahmad Mohamad Barakat (see profile above). Barakat and his fellow countryman Kalil Saleh established two import and export firms in Iquique—Saleh Trading Ltd. and Barakat Ltd.—in early June 2001. Another Lebanese, Arafat Ismail, an associate of Saleh, was running both businesses.[101] At that time, Chile's interior minister filed a request only for an investigation of the operations of several Lebanese business owners in Iquique, including Barakat and Ismail Alo Mohamed, who was banned from leaving the country because of his alleged connection with a network that finances Hizballah.

Santiago's *La Tercera de la Hora* reported in early November 2001 that detectives from the recently created International Affairs Unit of the Police Intelligence (Jipol) had detected at

---

[98] Nelson Fredy Padilla, "Los hombres de Osama bin Laden en Colombia," *Cromos*, No. 4, 364, September 24, 2001.

[99] "New Drug Gangs Spreading in Colombia," *The Global Intelligence Report* (Stratfor), April 3, 2002, citing *El Tiempo*.

[100] "Chile Confirms Alleged Terrorist-Linked Financial Network Under Investigation," FBIS, LAP20011109000089, November 9, 2001, translating Estrategia (a Santiago financial daily, Internet Version-WWW), November 9, 2001.

least two partnerships in which Barakat appears to be the main investor. The detectives determined that Saleh Trading Ltd was registered at an Iquique notary on June 6, 2001, with an initial capital of $50,000. A Chilean citizen participated in the partnership. The second partnership, the import and export company Barakat Ltd., was registered the following day at the same notary, with an initial capital of $20,000. Barakat, who gave El Arrecife Building, Apartment 902, Iquique, as his address, contributed $19,800 to the partnership with Juan Lecaros Figueroa.[102]

The company declared that its objective was to "import and export of all kinds of merchandise, especially clothes and electronic items, and to engage in any other business that the partners agree to, under the free zone area or the general customs regulations." Investigators cited by *La Tercera de la Hora*, however, confirmed that the money allegedly laundered in Iquique came from Ciudad del Este, using the businesses in Chile as a cover up. These activities could reach several million dollars.

Barakat acknowledged in an interview with a Chilean newspaper in November 2001 that he has businesses in Chile and the United States (Miami and New York). He also reiterated that he is "only a sympathizer" of Hizballah, which he sends "$400 a year to help the orphans of the south Lebanon liberation war."[103]

Colombia

In comparison with the Triborder Region, relatively little Islamic terrorist activity has been reported in Colombia, if this initial research is any indication. The occasional presence of an Islamic fundamentalist terrorist in Colombia has been reported. These may have been individuals attempting to visit with the Revolutionary Armed Forces of Colombia (FARC) or to travel on to Maicao, Colombia, or on to Margarita Island, Venezuela, where there are sizeable Arab communities.

---

[101] "Chilean Police Investigate Terrorist Financial Network," *Santiago Times*, January 8, 2002.

[102] Héctor Rojas and Pablo Vergara, *La Tercera de la Hora* [Santiago; a conservative, pro-business, top-circulation daily, Internet Version-WWWW], November 8, 2001, as translated in "Chilian Police Examine Link to Alleged Triborder Hizballah Financial Network," FBIS, LAP20011108000085, November 8, 2001.

[103] *La Tercera de la Hora* (Internet Version-WWW), November 14, 2001, as translated in FBIS LAP20011114000075200, "Hizballah-Linked Businessman Acknowledges Having Businesses in Chile, US," November 14, 2001.

The Arrest of an Islamic Jihad Terrorist in Colombia

Mohamed Abed Abdel Aal, a leader of the al Qaeda-affiliated Egyptian Islamic Jihad (Jamaa Islamiyya), was arrested in Colombia in October 1998. He had been in Italy under "surveillance," according to Colonel Germán Jaramillo Piedrahita, the head of Colombia's intelligence police, who was interviewed by Colombia's Radio Caracol on October 21, 1998. Abdel Aal is wanted by Egyptian authorities for his involvement in two terrorist massacres of tourists: the Jamaa Islamiyya terrorist attack in Luxor, Egypt on November 17, 1997, in which 62 people were killed; and in connection with an incident in which terrorists killed 20 Greek tourists by raking them with gunfire outside their Cairo hotel on April 18, 1996.

Jaramillo explained that sometime in 1998 Abdel Aal boarded a plane in Amsterdam bound for Ecuador because the Colombian consulate in Italy had denied him a visa to travel directly to Bogotá. Sometime during 1998, Abdel Aal reportedly had participated in transactions with Colombian guerrillas that involved arms, drugs, and money, and may have been returning to raise money.

Colombian Police arrested Mohamed Abed Abdel Aal on October 19, 1998, two days after he arrived in Bogotá by bus from Quito. He was subsequently deported to Ecuador. On arriving at Quito's Mariscal Airport, he was reportedly accompanied by three men who escorted him, without handcuffs, to an unidentified car, which left for an undisclosed location.[104] Abel Aal then mysteriously "disappeared."[105] He was later reportedly turned over to Egyptian authorities. It was not the first instance of Islamic Jihad terrorist activities in Colombia. In 1992 Interpol agents arrested seven alleged members of the Islamic Jihad in Quito, Ecuador. The agents claimed that they planned attacks on the Israeli ambassador in Bogotá, Colombia.

---

[104] "Egyptian Suspect in Luxor Attack Arrives in Ecuador," *The Daily Telegraph* [London], October 21, 1998.
[105] "Terrorist with Bin Laden Connections Arrested in Colombia," *Global Intelligence Update* (Stratfor online

Iranian Government Ties to the FARC

On December 22, 1999, the Iranian Embassy in Bogotá announced that Tehran has suspended construction of a meat-packing plant and slaughterhouse in Colombia's Demilitarized Zone. Colombian Defense Minister Luis Fernando Ramírez had expressed concern at the end of November that Iranian military advisers were part of the group installing the slaughterhouse, and that these Iranians were somehow connected to the FARC, which controlled the DMZ. An Iranian delegation first visited the area in June 1999, and an agreement was signed between the local government and the Islamic Republic on October 21, promptly raising suspicions about installation of a high-capacity facility in an area that cannot fulfill export requirements. Colombian officials suspected that Iranian interest in that immediate region could have been linked with the narcotics trade and the FARC.

Islamic Fundamentalist Ties to the FARC

Alleged links between the FARC and Islamic terrorist organizations is a subject that may need more in-depth investigation. There have been indications of linkage between the FARC and Hizballah or other Islamist groups that allegedly operate in the Triborder Region of Argentina, Brazil, and Paraguay.[106] In October 2000, Paraguayan counternarcotics police broke up an arms-for-cocaine ring between Paraguay and the FARC.[107] At that time, Paraguayan counternarcotics police arrested an individual believed to be representing the FARC for possible involvement in a guns-for-cocaine ring between Paraguay and the Colombian terrorist group.

At the beginning of 2001, Brazilian authorities received information from U.S. intelligence and crime fighting services saying that the FARC was supposedly trafficking drugs and weapons with Islamic extremists in the Triborder Region. The international cooperation between the FARC and al Qaeda was allegedly increasing as a result of the war in Afghanistan. One of the U.S. investigators told *O Globo* that "…it is very probable that there is an alliance

---

service), October 23, 1998.
[106] Comp. Samii A. William, "Iranians Out of Colombia," *Iran Report* [RFE/RL News], 2, December 7, 1999, [http://www.rferl.org/iran-report/1999/12/-271299.html], citing Spain's official EFE press agency.
[107] U.S. Department of State, *Patterns of Global Terrorism, 2000*, April 2001.

between the Taliban regime and bin Laden, who are taking part in this illegal trade with the Colombian traffickers to stimulate the production of heroin and serve the market."[108]

Suspected Hizballah Cells in Maicao

FBI investigators allegedly told Rio de Janeiro's *O Globo* in late October 2001 that, in addition to the Triborder Region, a focal point of terrorism in South America is Maicao, a little city of 58,000 residents in Colombia, close to the border with Venezuela. The free trade zone of Maicao, which has an Islamic community of 4,670, is known as a vacation spot for orthodox Islamics. Maicao's Islamic community, in which there are cells of the radical group Hizballah, controls 70 percent of the local commerce. "The merchants from there make contributions equivalent to 10 percent and even up to 30 percent of their profits. And those responsible for the fund send the money via banks in Maracaibo, Venezuela, and Panama. Sometimes part of it is carried personally by emissaries from those cells," a U.S. source told *O Globo*.[109]

The Arab community in Maicao, which has the necessary infrastructure to carry on its own cultural, commercial, educational, and social activities, is known to be the largest and best organized in Colombia. Approximately 8,000 people of Arab origin live in Maicao, the trade capital of La Guajira Department. Most of them belong to the Sunni or Shiite religious ethnic groups. The minority Shiites are reportedly more closely associated with the Muslim fundamentalist concept. With the exception of the closing by the Department of Administrative Security (Departamento de Seguridad Administrativa—DAS) of Radio Park, a clandestine radio station in Maicao, on August 15, 1997, for broadcasting Hizballah propaganda, and a couple of arrests for money laundering, Maicao's Muslim community reportedly has had few contacts with the law. Nevertheless, it is known that the black market for weapons and money laundering in Maicao and neighboring Zulia State in Venezuela is well established.

---

[108] "Brazil: Daily Notes US Views Triborder as Al-Qa'idah Center for L.A.," FBIS LAP20011029000036, October 29, 2001, translating José Meirelles Passos, "The Shadow of Bin Ladin in Latin America," *O Globo* (Internet Version-WWW), October 29, 2001.
[109] "Brazil: Daily Notes US Views Triborder as Al-Qa'idah Center for L.A.," FBIS LAP20011029000036, October 29, 2001, translating Jose Meirelles Passos, "The Shadow of Bin Ladin in Latin America," *O Globo* (Internet Version-WWW), October 29, 2001.

Hizballah cells based in Maicao have been using the networks that launder money from drug trafficking and contraband in Colombia to disguise money that will later be used to finance terrorist operations

worldwide, according to a

Colombian investigative

journalist.[110] According to

Colombian investigators,

nationalized Arabs who

serve as money-laundering

couriers have easily

obtained Colombian

citizenship because they

need only two witnesses to

testify that they were born

in Colombia.

In January 2000, intelligence officials In Colombia reportedly believed that another Egyptian terrorist suspect, Muhammad Ubayd Abd-al-Al, could be hiding in Maicao, according to *El Heraldo*. The suspect is "a member of an organization that works for al-Qa'ida," the paper said, and he is wanted by Egypt for involvement in an attempt to assassinate President Mubarak. An earlier report in *El Espectador* [Bogotá] stated that the Egyptian is a member of the Islamic Group, and cited Interpol's view that he is "very dangerous."[111]

Uruguay

A month after the bomb attack against the AMIA (Argentine-Israeli Mutual Association) building in Buenos Aires in July 1994, Brazilian government suspicion began focusing on the city of Chuí, Rio Grande do Sul State, in the southern part of Brazil, at the border with Uruguay.

---

[110] Fabio Castillo, with research by Leydi Herrera, "The Hizballah Contacts in Colombia," Part III of a special reportage entitled "Tracking the Tentacles of the Middle East in South America," published in the Investigative Reports section, *El Espectador* (Internet Version-WWW), December 9, 2001, as translated by FBIS, LAP20011210000036, "Alleged Hizballah Ties in Colombia Investigated," December 9, 2001.
[111] "Latin America: Islamic Fundamentalists in Colombia, Paraguay," FBIS LAP20020109000016; LAP20020109000081; LAP20011211000030 , January 10, 2002, citing the daily London Bureau roundup of terrorism issues/developments in the Mideast/Islamic world and the Aegean derived from sources monitored by FBIS.

It is easy to reach Buenos Aires from Chuy by sea, thereby avoiding border controls. Part of Chuy is in Uruguay, and part is in Brazil. Both parts of the city, each with about 18,000 residents, are divided by a wide avenue. The city has a total of about 1,500 Arab residents.

Citing official Brazilian government sources, Brazil's *O Globo* Television Network and newspaper reported on August 18, 1994, that a well-armed group belonging to the Islamic Unification Party and to the Amal and Hizballah groups had been detected in the Chuí zone. According to the Brazilian reports, a point of distribution of military weapons such as M-16 and AR-15, grenades, and rocket launchers was detected. Indignant, the Uruguayan government denounced the report, claiming that no subversives were living among the Arabs in Uruguay.[112]

The mayor of Chuí on the Brazilian side of the border, Mohammed Kasim (also spelled Kassem) Jomaa ("Mohamed Yoma") has been accused of being a Lebanese nationalist with strong connections to bin Laden and other Saudi terrorists. The Uruguayan secret service questioned the mayor, who allegedly helped Al Said Hassan Hussein Mukhlis' family after his arrest and visited him in jail. Porto Alegre's *Zero Hora* [Porto Alegre] of September 2, 2001, described Jomaa as the presumed chief of the emerging "Arab mafia," an organization involved in arms and drug trafficking, money laundering, and exploitation of undocumented workers.[113]

After the September 11 attacks, Jomaa was accused of being covertly in contact with Mukhlis, and having given shelter to his wife, Sahar (Sarrah) Mohamed Hassam Abud Hamanra. Federal Police forces of Brazil's Rio Grande do Sul State had been investigating Jomaa for supposed links to Mukhlis, whom he had visited in jail. Brazilian authorities appeared to be more concerned, however, with charges that Jomaa is a Lebanese citizen and therefore not eligible to

---

[112] "Brazilian Officials Warn Uruguay About Islamic Groups at Border," JPRS-TOT-94-036-L, September 1, 1994, 16.

[113] Enrique Medeot, "El alcalde brasileño que jura no ser amigo de Bin Laden" (The Brazilian Mayor Who Swears That He Isn't A Friend of bin Laden), Clarín.com, September 16, 2001.

hold the post of mayor in Brazil.[114] Jomaa denied any links with bin Laden, and claimed that he had aided Hamanra and her three children as a humanitarian gesture.

A confidential document obtained by *Zero Hora* says that "Every time that Mohamed [Jomaa] traveled to Lebanon, he had contact with Osama bin Laden in Afghanistan," and that bin Laden would be willing to contribute $2 million for the construction of a mosque in Chuí. According to a statement made by his mother, Nabihi Jomaa, in Lebanon to the Brazilian ambassador, the mayor was born on August 16, 1959, in the Lebanese city of Konaitra, which is today located in Syria. His Brazilian certificate, however, states that he was born on November 25, 1960, in São Paulo's Mooca district. Brazilian law requires that a mayor be born in Brazil.

Uruguayan investigations have found links between the Arab Mafia and the Lebanese Mafia, which operates in São Paulo, in connection with drug trafficking. According to the chief of police of Uruguay's Rocha Province, nearly 200 kilos of cocaine were hidden in Chuy and were smuggled to Europe via the port of Montevideo. The confidential Federal Police (PF) document states that "The money obtained from the sale of the product would be used to finance international terrorism."[115]

Venezuela
Suspected Hizballah/Al Qaeda Cells on Margarita Island

Like Maicao in Colombia, Margarita Island (Isla Margarita) is known as a vacation spot for orthodox Islamics. According to business reports, 80 percent of the businessmen in Margarita Island, a tourist center where sales are duty-free, are of Arab descent and arrived in Venezuela in the early 1980s.

There have been occasional reports of Islamic fundamentalists in the area. In 1996, according to *El Nacional* [Caracas], Venezuela's Directorate of Intelligence and Prevention Services (Dirección de Servicios de Inteligencia y Prevención—DISIP) discovered a 15-member cell of "Muslim radicals" who live in the tourist center of Margarita Island. According to the cited DISIP report, the cell included businessman Yousset Farhat (possibily related to the clan; see below).

---

[114] *New York Times*, September 27, 2001.
[115] Sérgo Gobetti, "PF investiga ligação de prefeito con Bin Laden" (PF Investigates Mayor's Links with bin Laden"), Oestadao.com.br, September 12, 2001.

In late January 1997, DISIP arrested two middle-age men—Wahid Mugnie and Ali Makke—in Porlamar, Margarita, alleged to be members of Hizballah. They had departed Lebanon in early 1997, after being denied entry visas by the Venezuelan Consulate in Lebanon because of their suspected Hizballah affiliation. They arrived in Buenos Aires on January 6, passed through Maicao on January 26, and then, having obtained visas from Venezuela's Directorate of Foreign Nationals, despite the Foreign Ministry's explicit instructions not to issue them, were flown directly to Margarita from Paraguachon, Guajira Department. [116] Another Lebanese national with suspected terrorist ties arrived in Margarita in late September 2001 and was arrested by the National Guard at the Santiago Marino International Airport moments before he was to board a flight to Puerto España. The individual, named "Ali Mamad Aman," was carrying a false Mexican passport.[117]

As of October 2001, an investigative commission of Venezuela's Judicial Technical Police (PTJ), consisting of four members of the PTJ and the International Police (Interpol) began to investigate bank accounts in Zulia State that might be tied to extremist groups, such as al Qaeda, and that have financed terrorist actions, including the attacks on the United States on September 11. The head of the PTJ homicide division, Captain Alejandro Hernández, stated that the homicide and Interpol divisions have already discovered that accounts have been opened in Venezuela containing large sums of money, and that there is a flow or exchange of this money going to certain islands and countries.

The Farhad Brothers' Hizballah-Linked Money-Laundering Operation

In late 2001, two clans, one of them headed by Syrian-Lebanese subject Mohamed Ali Farhad, who has been detained twice as a suspect in money-laundering investigations, were being investigated for operating a network that involves gun running and drug trafficking operations, as well as sending bank checks for huge amounts of money to Islamic fundamentalist groups, especially Hizballah. For example, Middle Eastern terrorists moved through the Colombia-based network part of the money to finance the attack on New York's World Trade Center on February 26, 1993. Farhad is a shareholder of a Margarita Island casino and owner of

---

[116] Javier Ignacio Mayorca, *El Nacional* [Caracas], January 31, 1997, as translated in "DISIP Arrests 2 Alleged Hezbollah Terrorists in Margarita," FBIS PA0102175297.

[117] Miriam Carolina Pérez, "GN detiene en Margarita a presunto terrorista" (GN Detains A Suspected Terrorist in Margarita), September 30, 2001; http://www.elnorte.com.ve/2001_septiembre/30/Sucesos432.html

the America textiles store. Colonel (ret.) Julio Andrade was quoted as saying that during the Sierra Carlos case, a link was established between the cigarette trade and two Arab clans in Maicao. Mohamed Ali Farhad ran the operation, which was worth $650 million.[118]

Three operations to combat money laundering conducted in 2001 in conjunction with Colombia's four intelligence services—the DAS and the Technical Investigation Corps (CTI) of the Office of the Prosecutor General—identified a Colombian member of the Cali Cartel ("Oscar Martínez") as the owner of a ship used to smuggle cocaine into Mexico and bring in weapons for the black market, which is controlled by one of the Arab clans operating in Maicao and Ipiales.

Following the September 11, 2001, attack on New York's World Trade Center Towers and Washington's Pentagon, the U.S. Department of State's list of international terrorists included the names of three individuals of Lebanese origin who reportedly live in Maicao but are believed to be hiding elsewhere in La Guajira Department.

According to unidentified sources consulted by *El Espectador*, at least one of the financial operations behind the 1993 World Trade Center bombing involved one of the clans that operate in Maicao.[119] Between March and October 1993, an individual named "Sinforoso Caballero," who was arrested in 1997, ran the Border Business Group and Cabadi Investments, which had been reportedly used to move the funds of the two Arab clans that operate in Maicao.

According to *El Espectador*, Mohamed Ali Farhad has been linked to a money laundering investigation that involved the Aruba-based Mansur clan of Eric and Alexander Mansur, who controlled cigarette smuggling in the 1990s through the Mansur Free Zone Trading Company N.V., with its main offices in the Netherlands Antilles.[120] The Mansurs inherited a smuggling and drug trafficking empire established in the islands by the Cosa Nostra's Cuntrera-Caruana clan, when it began to work in Venezuela with Cali Cartel organizations.

Until the U.S. indictment of the Mansur brothers for money laundering, Philip Morris' main

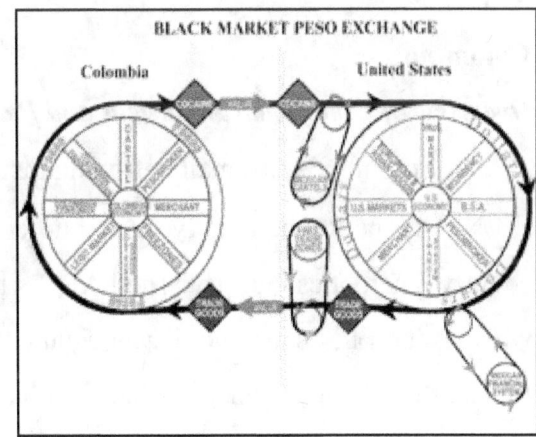

The black market peso exchange is a circuitous system by which drug dollars are laundered. For more information, visit http://www.treas.gov/fincen/advisu9.pdf.

---

[118] Vheadline.com (Venezuela), April 1, 2000.
[119] Castillo.
[120] Ibid.

distributor in Latin America was the Mansur Free Zone Trading Company, N.V.[121] According to a lawsuit filed against Philip Morris in 2000 by the governors of 25 of Colombia's 32 departments, plus the capital district of Bogotá, the company sold tobacco to smugglers in exchange for narco dollars, in what is commonly referred to as the Black Market Peso Exchange (BMPE). "Instead of repatriating narco dollars from their U.S. sales points, money launderers simply use them to purchase goods, which are then exported to Colombia and other Latin American countries and sold for pesos," according to the lawsuit. "The pesos then flow into the Colombian bank accounts of the drug barons."Allegedly, much of the proceeds garnered by the Mansur brothers went to Hizballah.

INDIGENOUS NARCO-TERRORIST GROUPS OPERATING IN LATIN AMERICA

A discussion of drug trafficking by Latin American guerrilla or terrorist groups necessarily focuses on Colombia's Revolutionary Armed Forces of Colombia (FARC), National Liberation Army (ELN), and United Self-Defense Groups of Colombia (AUC) and Peru's Shining Path. Although indigenous Latin American insurgent organizations such as Peru's Shining Path have been diminished, several others—such as Colombia's United Self-Defense Forces of Colombia (Autodefensas Unidas de Colombia—AUC) paramilitary groups, the FARC, and the ELN—still pose a dangerous threat to the region's stability.

Colombia

Overview of Colombian Insurgent and Paramilitary Involvement in the Drug Trade

Colombia's two main left-wing insurgent organizations—the National Liberation Army (ELN) and the Revolutionary Armed Forces of Colombia (FARC)—are heavily involved in the country's narcotics industry. The FARC's involvement probably began in the late 1980s, whereas the ELN's may not have begun until the late 1990s. The drug trade provides most of the finances for the hemisphere's oldest and largest guerrilla/terrorist group, the FARC, which exerts influence over a large area in southern Colombia. In earlier decades, the FARC financed itself

---

[121] *Tobacco Companies Linked to Criminal Organizations in Cigarette Smuggling: Latin America*, The Public i: An Investigative Report of the Center for Public Integrity, March 3, 2001.

mainly through extortion and kidnapping for ransom, but by the early 1990s it obtained 62 percent of its income from the drug industry.[122]

Political scientist Patricia Bibes quotes one Colombian military officer who pointed out that "FARC devotes 37 fronts, some 2,800 men (50 percent of its force), to drug-trafficking activities, and the Ejército de Liberación Nacional (ELN) seven fronts, some 500 men (20 percent of its force."[123] According to other Colombian military information, at least 32 of the FARC's 61 fronts, seven of the ELN's 41 fronts, and eight of the AUC's 19 fronts are known to derive income from the drug trade.[124]

Some elements of the FARC have gone beyond merely "taxing" the drug trade and have taken direct steps to control local base markets. At least one FARC unit has served as a cocaine source of supply for at least one international drug trafficking organization. According to Drug Enforcement Administration (DEA) administrator Asa Hutchinson, the FARC controls large areas of Colombia's eastern lowlands and rain forest—the country's primary coca-cultivation and cocaine-processing regions.

The ELN operates primarily along Colombia's northeastern border with Venezuela and in central and northwestern Colombia, including Colombia's cannabis and opium poppy-growing areas. The more ideological ELN was more reluctant than the FARC to exploit the drug trade. After the death of ELN ideologist Father Manuel Pérez in 1998, however, the ELN became more involved in the trade.[125] It has occasionally collaborated with the FARC to limit expansion by paramilitary forces in drug-producing regions. For example, in September 1998 the ELN and FARC joined

---

[122] "Steady Growth with Tidy Profits: Armed Struggle Has Its Compensation for Some," *Latin America Weekly Reports* [London], August 3, 1995, 8.

[123] Patricia Bibes, "Colombia: The Military and the Narco-Conflict," *Low Intensity Conflict & Law Enforcement*, 9, No. 1, Spring 2000, 41.

[124] According to Colombian analyst Alfredo Rangel Suárez, as cited by Angel Rabasa and Peter Chalk *Colombian Labyrinth: The Synergy of Drugs and Insurgency and its Implications for Regional Stability* (Santa Monica, California: Rand, 2001), 32, citing Table 3.1, "Links of illegal Armed Groups to the Drug Trade."

[125] According to Colombian analyst Alfredo Rangel Suárez, as cited by Rabasa and Chalk, 33.

forces to fight paramilitary groups in the San Lucas Mountains. The conflict related to control over territory in a region enriched by gold reserves and substantial coca growth.

The right-wing paramilitary organization known as the AUC (United Self Defense Forces of Colombia), an umbrella group that includes many Colombian paramilitary forces, has also maintained a significant stake in the drug trade, expanding its influence from its traditional base in the north to many areas in the coca-rich south that were previously controlled by the FARC.[126] The AUC and the Peasant Self-Defense Groups of Córdoba and Urabá (Autodefensas Campesinas de Córdoba y Urabá—ACCU) are right-wing paramilitary groups that emerged in the late 1980s to protect the interests of the regional elites, with the subtle backing of the Colombian military. Their emergence only exacerbated the conflict. The AUC has admitted earning up to 70 percent of its income from the drug trade. DEA administrator Hutchinson noted in his March 13, 2002, congressional testimony that several self-defense groups raise funds through extortion, or by protecting laboratory operations in northern and central Colombia.

Bibes notes that "Interestingly, the right-wing paramilitaries, also known as *autodefensas* [self-defense forces] in Colombia, are alleged to have strong ties to the drug trade as well as to the security forces."[127] According to classified DAS document cited by Bibes, Colombia's top paramilitary leader, Carlos Castaño, is well known as a drug trafficker.[128] Bibes points out that the FARC, in order to sell drugs and arms to the Caribbean and Panama, has been actively trying to open a corridor in a region that produces crops to finance the paramilitaries.

Official U.S. Views on Drug Financing of Colombian Terrorists

Phillip T. Chicola, director of Andean Affairs at the U. S. Department of State, commented in a December 4, 2000, Carnegie Council discussion that 60 to 90 percent of the funding for paramilitaries and guerrillas in Colombia comes from narco-trafficking. In his view, eliminating this major source of funding would decrease the level of violence in Colombia to a fraction of what it is now. Considering, however, that the level of violence in Colombia prior to the involvement of the insurgent and paramilitary forces in drug trafficking was just as high, if not higher, Chicola may be overly optimistic to assume that eliminating drug funding would

---

[126] U.S. Department of State. Office of the Coordinator for Counterterrorism, *Patterns of Global Terrorism, 2000*, April 30, 2001.
[127] Ibid.
[128] Ibid, 41-2.

solve the problem of political violence in Colombia. The guerrillas and paramilitaries would still be able to derive large amounts of operating revenue from kidnappings for ransom and extortion, including taxation of ranchers and farmers and petroleum companies for protection. In 1998 alone, for example, the revenue of Colombia's guerrilla and paramilitary organizations totaled $311 million from extortion and $236 million from kidnappings, according to Colombian government estimates.[129]

As presented to the Senate Committee on the Judiciary on March 13, 2002, the official U.S. Government view of the FARC's narcotics involvement is that many FARC units throughout southern Colombia raise funds through the extortion ("taxation") of both legal and illegal businesses, the latter including the drug trade. Similarly, in return for cash payments, or possibly in exchange for weapons, some FARC units protect cocaine laboratories and clandestine airstrips in southern Colombia. In addition, some FARC units may be independently involved in limited cocaine laboratory operations. Some FARC units in southern Colombia are more directly involved in local drug trafficking activities, such as controlling local cocaine base markets.

In response to the clear and substantial evidence of involvement in narcotics trafficking by the Colombian insurgent groups, U.S. Ambassador to Colombia Anne Patterson stated at a conference in Cartagena in late October 2001 that the United States requires the extraditions of the leaders of the AUC (because of its participation in drug trafficking), the ELN, and the FARC.[130] On March 18, 2002, the U.S. Department of Justice announced indictments on drug trafficking charges of three members of the FARC, including Tomás Medina Caracas (see image), two other Farc members, another Colombian, and three Brazilians. The indictment says "they sold cocaine for money and weapons, with the drugs bound for the US, Brazil, Suriname, Paraguay, Mexico, and Spain."[131]

---

[129] Rabasa and Chalk, 32, citing information from a Colombian Armed Forces briefing held in March 2000.
[130] *El Tiempo* [Bogotá], October 14, 2001.
[131] Nancy Dunne and James Wilson, "FARC Members Indicted in US," BBC Monitoring Service [UK], March 19, 2002.

The official U.S. government view of the ELN's involvement in narcotics was also presented to the U.S. Senate Committee on the Judiciary on March 13, 2002. This view holds that the territories under ELN influence—primarily along Colombia's northeastern border with Venezuela and in central and northwestern Colombia—include cannabis and opium poppy-growing areas. Some ELN units raise
funds through extortion or by
protecting laboratory operations.
Although some ELN units may be
independently involved in limited
cocaine laboratory operations, the ELN
appears to be much less dependent than
the FARC on coca and cocaine profits
to fund its operations. Despite its
expression of disdain for illegal drugs,
the ELN takes advantage of the profits
available where it controls coca-
producing areas.

Also as presented to the Senate
Committee on the Judiciary on March
13, 2002, the official U.S. Government
view of the AUC is that it admittedly uses the cocaine trade to finance its counterinsurgency campaign. The AUC's head, Carlos Castaño, stated in 2000 that "70 percent" of the AUC's operational funding was from drug money, and he described it as an undesired but necessary evil. AUC elements appear to be directly involved in processing cocaine and exporting cocaine from Colombia. In 2001, the AUC claimed publicly that it was getting out of the drug business. Nevertheless, it is not considered likely that the AUC's many semiautonomous units will voluntarily give up their lucrative drug business.

Revenues Derived From the Drug Trade

Estimates on the amount of funds that the ELN, FARC and paramilitary groups obtain from the drug trade vary widely. On August 3, 2001, the *Houston Chronicle* quoted Alfredo

Rangel, a Colombian military analyst, as saying that profits from the drug trade now make up 48 percent of the FARC's total income, amounting to nearly $180 million annually.[132] According to Colombian government estimates, in 1998 the revenue of Colombia's guerrilla and paramilitary organizations from the drug trade totaled $551 million. Others say the figure runs higher. Rafael Pardo, for example, explains that the FARC took control of Colombia's coca crops in the second half of the 1990s "and boosted its income to more than $600 million a year, making it possibly the richest insurgent group in history."[133]

According to Bibes, the Colombian guerrillas' involvement in illicit drug production and drug trafficking has remained focused primarily on the taxation of coca growers and cocaine production laboratories. She notes that, according to a study by the DEA, the FARC does not process and export cocaine to the United States.[134] By the early 1990s, moreoever, one-third of the FARC's revenues was reportedly coming from poppies.[135]

The DEA reported on July 9, 1997, that the FARC factions raise funds by providing security services to traffickers and charging a fee for each gallon of precursor chemicals and each kilo of coca leaf and cocaine HCL moving in their region. Some of these groups have assisted the drug traffickers by storing and transporting cocaine and marijuana within Colombia, and certain FARC units in Colombia may be engaged in localized opiate trafficking.

Klaus Nyholm of the U.N. Drug Control Programme in Colombia has noted that in some areas, autonomous FARC fronts are heavily involved with cocaine processing and export, whereas FARC fronts in other areas have no such involvement.[136] Of those FARC fronts that are involved, the units provide protection to coca growers and traffickers in return for a tax estimated at between 10 and 15 percent of the drug's value. Raúl Reyes, a high-ranking FARC official, explained to the *Washington Post*: "We charge them a tax. We don't do them any favors, and they don't do us any. Where the economic base is coca... that's what we tax—not the traffickers directly, but their intermediaries. In other regions we tax the cattle ranchers, the sugar growers, the businesses."[137]

---

[132] John Otis "Is the FARC a Drug Cartel?" *Houston Chronicle*, August 3, 2001.
[133] Rafael Pardo, "Colombia's Two-Front War," *Foreign Affairs*, July/August 2000, 70.
[134] Ibid.
[135] "The Guerrillas' Big Business," *Semana* [Bogotá], July 7, 1993, 26-32.
[136] "FARC: Finance Comes Full Circle for Bartering Revolutionaries," *Jane's Terrorism & Security Monitor*, January 6, 2001.
[137] Karen DeYoung, "For Rebels, It's Not a Drug War," *Washington Post*, April 10, 2000, A16.

More specifically, the FARC has a schedule of fees (*gramaje*) for providing protection and services to drug growers and traffickers. According to the Colombian Armed Forces, in October 1999 the FARC charged $15.70 for every kilo of basic paste produced by cocaine laboratories, $52.60 per kilo for production of chlorhydrate of cocaine, $5,263 per laboratory for protection, $52.60 per hectare for protection of coca fields, $4,210 per hectare for protection of poppy fields, $2,631 each for security of landing strips, $10.50 per kilo for protection of cocaine shipments, 20 percent of shipment value for river transportation of precursor chemicals, $5,263 each for protection of international drug flights, and $2,631 each for protection of domestic drug flights.[138] Increasingly, however, the FARC receives payment in cocaine. According to Nyholm, the trend for the FARC to receive payment in cocaine has deepened the organization's involvement in the drug business.

The huge revenues derived from the drug trade have allowed the Colombian guerrilla and paramilitary forces to become some of the best-funded in the world. In the second half of the 1990s, membership in the FARC and ELN reportedly increased threefold as a result of drug revenues.[139] Whereas the average per capita income in Colombia in 1995 was $1,800, the average annual guerrilla salary was, according to a British newsletter, $65,000.[140] Although it seems unlikely that the average annual guerrilla salary is anywhere near $65,000, there is little doubt that the Colombian guerrillas earn at least double the pay of soldiers. According to Leonardo Gallego, head of Colombia's antidrug police, the guerrillas can pay their troops the equivalent of $300 to $400 a month, while professional soldiers in the Colombian army make a little more than $200 a month.[141]

The Symbiotic Relationship Between the Guerrilla/Paramilitary Forces and the Drug Cartels

Despite their extensive involvement in the drug trade, it should not be assumed that the AUC, ELN, and FARC are close partners of the country's drug cartels. One analyst, James R. Van de Velde, notes that the approximately 12,000 to 15,000 guerrilla combatants in Colombia

---

[138] Rabasa and Chalk, 32-33.
[139] David Scanlan, "Colombian Rebels Cost Nation $12.5 Billion since 1990, Study Finds," *Bloomberg Business News*, January 1996, 2.
[140] Ibid.
[141] John Otis.

"...maintain weak links to the cocaine trafficking organizations."[142] As Patricia Bibes explains, the guerrillas and drug traffickers support each other's interests: "The guerrillas provide security assistance and defense to the drug traffickers, and the drug traffickers provide financial aid to the guerrillas in return." By the second half of the 1990s, Van de Velde explains, the ELN, the FARC, and the Popular Liberation Army (Ejército Popular de la Liberación—EPL), a Maoist guerrilla group that has since signed a peace agreement with the government, were "...involved in providing protection for drug traffickers and growers in exchange for payment or weapons. They also 'tax' drug farmers and traffickers in the territory they control."[143] Indeed, according to Van de Velde, "Drug trafficking and protection have become the guerrillas' principal source of financial support."[144] The services that the FARC performs for the drug traffickers, Van de Velde points out, include "protection, smuggling and paid violence against the government, to earn money to continue its operations."[145] He explains further:

> FARC operations with drug traffickers are often coordinated to avoid local law enforcement and international interdiction efforts. They work together with the traffickers to advance more sophisticated smuggling schemes and multiply smuggling opportunities. In exchange for weapons and financial support, the FARC will protect clandestine drug-related airfields, warn traffickers of impending police or military activity and protect coca plantations and processing laboratories. The FARC often carries out attacks on behalf of the traffickers, attacking organizations and individuals involved in drug interdiction.[146]

---

[142] James R. Van de Velde, "The Growth of Criminal Organizations and Insurgent Groups Abroad Due to International Drug Trafficking," *Low Intensity Conflict & Law Enforcement*, 5, No. 3, Winter 1996, 470.
[143] Ibid, 471.
[144] Ibid.
[145] Ibid, 472.
[146] Ibid, 472.

Under this symbiotic relationship, the coca growers are given protection while the guerrillas are provided with a source of revenue and recruits, the latter from among the peasant workers involved in coca or poppy cultivation. In addition, Van de Velde points out that the FARC terrorizes the rural population in general to compel cooperation with drug traffickers. In short, although the guerrilla and drug-trafficking organizations have a mutually beneficial relationship, it is a pragmatic, business-like one, and they keep each other at arm's length.

Drug Production in Guerrilla- or Paramilitary-Controlled Territory

In December 1998, when the government ordered the withdrawal of the army and the police from a Switzerland-size safe haven (referred to as the *despeje* or demilitarized zone (DMZ), to facilitate dialogue with the FARC, there were, officially recorded, 6,300 hectares planted with coca throughout the 42,000 square-kilometer (16,000-square-mile) DMZ and no signs of poppy plantations. During the peace negotiations, Colombian authorities began to receive information linking some of the FARC fronts with the handling of illegal crops and the processing and marketing of coca base in the DMZ. In May 2000, the security organizations accused the FARC of issuing special permits to buyers of coca base to enter the DMZ and at the same time imposing the prices of the sales.

In 2000 Colombia had more than 400,000 acres dedicated to coca, offsetting eradication efforts and leaving the size of the coca crop unchanged, according to United Nations' estimates. In that year, coca cultivation within the *despeje*, until

its official dissolution in February 2002, rose from 6,000 hectares to 7,900 hectares, according to the U.S. Embassy. This area accounted for 6 percent of overall Colombian cultivation. Most of the increase was the result of expansion in that portion of the Guaviare growing area that extended into the *despeje*, while the Macarena growing area, which is totally within the former FARC enclave, increased only by 300 hectares.

General Gustavo Socha, the director of the Counternarcotics Police, was quoted by BBC Monitoring Service in mid-March 2002 as stating:

> In this area [Vistahermosa, Mesetas, and San Vicente] and throughout the [former] demilitarized zone in general, not a single [coca] leaf was moved without the approval of the guerrillas. What really caught our attention was the fact that the increase in the amount of land planted occurred relatively close to the municipalities over which they had very strict control. Therefore, we are proving that what was always said regarding the increase in production and about the participation of the FARC in the business is true.[147]

The aerial survey located approximately 30 landing strips in the DMZ. General Socha pointed out that the guerrillas had prepared the landing strips to accommodate different types of aircraft. "Now we know that planes carrying chemicals, weapons and money landed here and took off with shipments of cocaine. If, as we believe, the FARC harvested the crops of the last two years, it would not be mad to think that about 80 tons of the alkaloid were processed in this region," General Socha told *Cambio*.[148]

In October 2001, six Colombian governmental entities that are part of the Integrated System for Monitoring Illicit Crops (Simci) received a complete report, according to which the areas planted with illegal crops had increased throughout the DMZ.[149] Maps drafted on the basis of the information provided by commercial satellite surveys and photographs taken from special aircraft left no doubt that the coca crops covered an area 16,000 hectares. This information showed that 12 percent of all the illegal crops reported by the satellites are within the DMZ and, according to official figures released in October 2001, the 12 percent amounts to 144,600 hectares.

The satellite signals also showed that in southern Caquetá, outside the DMZ and near the municipalities of Cartagena del Chaira and Remolinos del Caguán, a further 7,500 hectares are planted with coca. According to government sources, the existence of these plantations now

---

[147] "Colombia: Investigations Show FARC Controlled Drug Crops, Trafficking in Ex-DMZ," BBC Monitoring Service [UK], March 15, 2002.
[148] *Cambio* web site [Bogotá], Mar 11, 2002.
[149] "Los cultivos de las FARC" (The FARC's Crops), Revista Cambio.com, March 11, 2002.

explains the FARC's previous interest in expanding the DMZ to those towns. The maps show that the biggest concentration of coca and poppies are not far from the urban areas of La Macarena and Vistahermosa, even though plantations are also visible in areas a bit further from Uribe, Mesetas, and San Vicente del Caguán.

The FARC's Opium Production

The FARC is also believed to be involved in opium poppy cultivation. The satellite images contained in the October 2001 report also showed the existence of 420 hectares planted with poppies. After the Taliban fundamentalist regime in Afghanistan banned poppy production, the drug cartels began to seek new suppliers. Afghani and Pakistani drug traffickers arrived in Colombia, contacted the Cali Cartel, and taught them how to grow and process poppy until it is converted into heroin. General José Cadena, a former Colombian police chief, commented that:

> The ones who brought this problem [to Colombia] were Afghanis and Pakistanis. They entered with tourist visas through Peru, Ecuador, and Bolivia, and here they worked giving instructions for planting.… They are the ones who taught the Cali Cartel to plant poppy.

Most of Colombia's opium poppy crop can be found in the departments of Tolima and Huila in south-central Colombia and adjacent to the Venezuelan border in the Perijá Mountains of northern Colombia. Although Colombia is the largest cultivator of opium poppies in South America, its crop has traditionally only accounted for about 2 percent of worldwide potential opium production. Colombian police sources have warned that dozens of Afghans using false Pakistani passports have been involved in developing illegal poppy cultivations to make heroin. Former police chief General Rosso José Serrano observed that "Poppy growths recently uncovered in Colombia are planted in long rows similar to the growing methods detected in Afghanistan."[150] As with coca growing and cocaine production, the FARC reportedly is also involved in taxing opium poppy cultivation.

---

[150] Martin Arostegui, "Search for Bin Laden Links Looks South," www.autentico.org [UPI via COMTEX], October 12, 2001.

Counternarcotics Operations

Rural

According to a July 9, 1997, DEA report, Colombian National Police helicopters and planes used in drug-eradication efforts continually receive ground fire when conducting counterdrug operations. Guerilla groups provide security for and aggressively defend coca and poppy fields and the processing laboratories, such as the huge HCL conversion complex seized in January 1997. The FARC has also aggressively defended its drug interests on the ground. For example, in August 1998 FARC forces attacked the counternarcotics base at Miraflores.

According to the *International Narcotics Control Strategy Report, 2001*, in 2001 Joint Task Force South (JTFS) operations were directed at all drug-producing and -trafficking groups, both guerrilla and paramilitary. In May 2001, Colombia's Counternarcotics Brigade units clashed with AUC forces in Caquetá that had been engaged in drug-trafficking activity and extortion of the local populace. JTFS forces destroyed 20 cocaine HCl labs, 700 coca base labs, 167 kilos of cocaine HCl, and 2,951 kilos of coca base. They seized 291,603 gallons of liquid precursor chemicals, 406,914 kilos of solid precursor chemicals, 117 vehicles, and a great deal of drug processing equipment such as microwave ovens.

In August-September 2001, the Counternarcotics Brigade dealt a serious blow to the FARC's drug-trafficking infrastructure in Putumayo near the Ecuador border. In this area, which is a center of operations for the FARC's

48th Front and a key drug corridor for the movement of precursor chemicals, drugs, arms, and explosives to and from neighboring Ecuador, the Brigade destroyed a FARC-operated oil refinery capable of producing 2,000 gallons of gasoline a day for use exclusively in the production of coca base. The Counternarcotics Brigade also identified and destroyed a FARC-built 40-kilometer road potentially used to transport drugs, weapons, and essential chemicals to and from Ecuador, and in addition destroyed seven abandoned FARC base camps along the corridor. In a joint Counternarcotics

Brigade-12th Brigade operation in a stronghold held by the three FARC fronts most heavily involved in drug trafficking, JTFS forces destroyed several more abandoned FARC base camps.[151]

After suspending peace negotiations with the FARC and entering the FARC's former safe haven (*despeje*) on February 20, 2002, the Colombian Armed Forces found numerous cocaine complexes in the FARC's neutral, demilitarized zone in the south.[152] In late March, the Colombian Army also discovered and destroyed a FARC complex for the production of cocaine, located in Puerto Asís, Putumayo Department, on the southwestern border with Ecuador. The complex consisted of 31 laboratories, according to military officials. The army raid destroyed 35,000 liters of liquid products and 12,000 kilos of solid items for preparing cocaine. The complex had the capacity for producing about 500 kilos of alkaloid monthly.

Five days after the Colombian Army occupied the urban areas of the five municipalities within the DMZ (the FARC's *despeje*) on February 22, 2002, four counternarcotics police officers in a National Police phantom aircraft silently

flew over the former DMZ region to confirm the existence in the DMZ of vast areas planted with coca and poppies. The armed forces began crop-spraying operations on March 3. While the DMZ had been under FARC control, crop spraying was too risky to attempt. Satellite images led the authorities to estimate that the former DMZ zone contains about 15,000 hectares of coca plants used to manufacture cocaine, and between 400 and 500 hectares of opium poppy plants used in the production of heroin.[153] The

---

[151] U.S. Department of State, Bureau for International Narcotics and Law Enforcement Affairs, *International Narcotics Control Strategy Report, 2001*, March 1, 2002.

[152] "Ejército destruye complejo cocalero de las Farc en Putumayo" (Army Destroys FARC Cocaine Complex in Putumayo), *El Tiempo* [Bogotá], March 30, 2002.

[153] Jenny Manrique, *El Espectador* [Bogotá], March 2, 2002, as cited in "Coca Eradication to Begin in Former Colombian Demilitarized Zone," BBC Monitoring Service [UK], March 4, 2002.

poppies were planted on the slopes of a mountain range at heights of between 1,800 meters and 2,500 meters above sea level.

Urban

According to authorities, an amount totaling almost half a million dollars, including $135,000 in U.S. dollars, and accounting and financial reports presumably belonging to the FARC's 16th Front, were confiscated in raids carried out against bank branches in Bogotá on April 10, 2002. "This is a product of narcotrafficking," General Reinaldo Castellanos, commander of the Army's 13th Brigade, stated. "These financial aspects are precisely narcotrafficking business."[154] The investigators found that part of the funds was apparently managed by Germán Briceño Suárez ("Grannobles"), the brother of Jorge Briceño ("El Mono Jojoy"), the FARC's military commander.

The combined army-fiscal police operation came a week after the capture in Tunja of two individuals who were transporting $450,000 in cash hidden in a truck. According to Justo Pastor Rodríguez, the national finance director, the results of the operation showed that the FARC managed a central account in seven houses located in northern Bogotá, where it laundered money that exceeded $20 million and controlled the money that it would receive from the 16th Front's narcotrafficking operational units.[155]

The FARC's Brazilian Mafia Connection

In March 2001, the Colombian Armed Forces undertook Operation Gato Negro in southeastern Colombia. The operation revealed the Colombian guerrillas' ties with narcotraffickers of Brazil, Mexico, Venezuela, and the United States, according to Defense Minister Luis Fernando Ramírez.[156] The two-month antinarcotics effort culminated with the capture of Brazil's most notorious drug trafficker, Fernando Da Costa ("Fernandinho Beira-Mar"), 33, on April 21, 2001. Colombian Army officials said that the event highlighted connections between Da Costa's organization and the FARC. Da Costa was arrested in the Colombian jungle after a manhunt by 300 army troops, who eventually cornered him in Vichada

---

[154] "Descubren central contable de las Farc" (FARC's Central Account Discovered), *El Espectador* [Bogotá], April 11, 2002.
[155] Ibid.

Province near the Venezuelan border. Top Colombian Army officials have maintained that Da Costa had been selling arms to leftist rebels of the FARC, in exchange for cocaine.

Until his capture, Brazil's arms-for-cocaine trafficking revolved around Da Costa, known as Brazil's Pablo Escobar. Brazil's Parliamentary Commission, after investigating narcotics trafficking in Brazil, identified Da Costa as one of the major Brazilian mafia chiefs, with international connections in Paraguay, Peru, and Colombia. With the contacts that he made in Paraguay during his 13 years of residency in that country, Da Costa purchased arsenals there and brought them to Barranco Minas (Guainía). He maintained his base of operations in Paraguay until forced to move to Colombia. Brazilian authorities established that Da Costa had connections with 53 people in Brazil through bank accounts in different countries of the world.

Captured by Brazilian authorities in 1996, Da Costa escaped from prison in Minas de Gerais nine months later, in March 1997, after paying police authorities and guards several million dollars. He then returned to Paraguay, where he reunited with the Morel family, which heads Paraguay's drug trafficking,[157] and began operating out of the Paraguayan town of Pedro Juan Caballero. His brother, Marcelo, who was also captured in Brazil, and Ney Machada, who had cells in Colombia, Paraguay, and Brazil and who was arrested in Colombia's Operation Gato Negro, had been in charge of drug shipments to Brazil, Suriname, and Paraguay.[158]

In February 2001, the army arrested several Brazilians and confiscated documents that officials said showed how the rebels received arms from Da Costa in exchange for a Brazilian-bound shipment of cocaine. Colombian authorities extradited Da Costa to Brazil on April 24, 2001.

---

[156] "Gobierno colombiano confirma nexos FARC-narcos mexicanos," *La Crónica de Hoy* [Mexico], March 29, 2001.
[157] "El prontuario de Fernandinho" (Fernandiño's Handbook), *El Tiempo*, April 21, 2001.
[158] "Muestran a Fernandiño a la prensa" (Fernandiño Shown to the Press), *El Tiempo* [Bogotá], April 22, 2001.

After the capture of Da Costa, the commander of the Colombian Armed Forces, General Fernando Tapias Stahelin, revealed on April 23, 2001, that "there were connections between the fugitive and Vladimiro Montesinos, the security advisor for the former Peruvian president Alberto Fujimori, in regard to arms trafficking to the FARC." The general was referring specifically to the shipment of 10,000 AK-47s sent to the FARC by the Russian mafia in 2000.[159] General Tapias affirmed that Da Costa had delivered "10,000 arms and 3 million cartridges" to the FARC.[160] MSNBC.com, citing U.S. intelligence officials, reported that the Russian mafia/FARC arms-for-drugs ring had been operational for two years. MSNBC.com first broke the story of large arms shipments to FARC rebels in October 1999. That shipment drew the attention of U.S. intelligence agencies to what they eventually concluded was a major trafficking ring. That single airdrop in October 1999 was said by U.S. intelligence officials to have delivered $50 million worth of AK-47s deep inside FARC-held territory.

According to MSNBC.com, citing U.S. intelligence, Da Costa had been running arms received from Fuad Jamil, a Lebanese businessman operating in the same Paraguayan town. The official said Jamil uses a legitimate import company as a front. Although most of the weaponry goes directly to FARC, a smaller amount is parceled off to other groups. Among them is Hizballah. According to MSNBC.com, U.S. intelligence officials say Hizballah has ties with the Arab immigrant communities of Paraguay, Ecuador, Venezuela, and Brazil, and frequently uses legitimate business operations to cover illegal arms transfers.

According to General Fernando Tapias, Da Costa told investigators after his arrest that the rebels control nearly every facet of the drug trade in Colombia's eastern jungles. The rebels, Tapias added, helped Da Costa export more than 200 tons of cocaine to Brazil during 2000-01, receiving $500 for each kilogram of the drug and $15,000 for every narcotics flight that left the area.

---

[159] Luis Esnal, "Nexos con Montesinos" (Nexus with Montesinos), *La Nación* [Buenos Aires], April 24, 2001, 2.

FARC Connections with Other Drug-Trafficking Cartels

Mexican authorities provided proof of the FARC's narcotics trafficking when they captured Carlos Ariel Charry ("El Doctór"), a Colombian physician from San Vicente del Caguán. Charry travelled to Mexico as an emissary for FARC military commander Jorge Briceño ("Mono Jojoy") allegedly to do business with the Tijuana Cartel. When Charry was arrested in Mexico City in early November 2000, the authorities found that he was carrying a videotape that showed him with the FARC's military leader, who introduced him as his envoy to conduct coca-for-weapons transactions with the Tijuana Cartel.

With the arrest of Dr. Carlos Ariel Charry Guzmán and Mexican Enrique Guillermo Salazar Ramos in Juárez, Mexico, Mexican authorities believed they had the middlemen in a relationship between the Tijuana Cartel of the Arellano-Félix family and the FARC.[161] The arrests yielded evidence that the FARC supplied cocaine to the cartel in exchange for money and possibly weapons.

Peru

Shining Path Involvement in the Narcotics Trade: Background

As presented to the U.S. Senate Committee on the Judiciary on March 13, 2002, the official U.S. Government view of the Shining Path's narcotics involvement is that the Shining Path (Sendero Luminoso—SL), a Maoist terrorist organization, historically has operated in remote areas of Peru where drug producers, drug traffickers, and terrorists can operate largely without interference by security or military forces. In these areas, the SL has used violence to protect safe havens and protection and extortion rackets involving coca and cocaine. According to the *International Narcotics Control Strategy Report, 2001*, the governments of Peru and the United States believe that the Shining Path "continues to be involved in protection of coca crops and possibly narcotics production and trafficking."[162]

The SL's terrorism campaign during the 1980s and the first half of the 1990s was largely funded by levies that it imposed on cocaine trafficking. As the SL waned in the late 1990s, so did

---

[160] Eleonora Gosman, "Temen una guerra entre bandas de narcos en Brasil" (Cartel Wars Are Feared), *Clarín*.com, April 24, 2001.
[161] "The FARC-Tijuana Axis," *Foreign Report* [London], December 7, 2000.

its influence on the drug trade. But in 2001, the SL had a slight resurgence in areas like the Huallaga and Apurímac valleys, where coca is cultivated and processed, indicating that the remnants of the group are probably financing operations with drug profits from security and taxation "services."

The Shining Path began political work in the upper Huallaga Valley in 1980 and by 1982 began building an organization in the region, according to José E. Gonzales.[163] According to author Simon Strong, the SL moved into the coca-producing Upper Huallaga Valley of Peru in the second half of 1983, and by mid-1984 Colombian drug traffickers had begun terrorizing the valley's coca growers.[164] The SL was able to offer the campesinos protection against exploitation by Colombian and Peruvian drug trafficking gangs and U.S. and Peruvian counternarcotics efforts and succeeded in ending the Colombian drug traffickers' dominance by the mid-1980s.[165] Strong explains that "The party [SL] does not market coca: As an aspirant state, it taxes the trade by way of requesting collaboration money from it as well as other businesses."[166] By the early 1990s, Strong points out, the SL had apparently failed to purchase any sophisticated weapons in Peru or abroad despite the millions of dollars it had earned by eliciting protection money for flights by drug traffickers as well as "collaboration cash from the peasants, intermediary traffickers, travelers, and businessmen...." Moreover, he contends that any relationship between the SL and the drug traffickers "has never been proved."[167] (By "relationship," Strong presumably means close ties.)

The relationship between the Maoist-oriented SL and the profit-driven drug traffickers was a pragmatic but often violent one in the late 1980s and early 1990s. As long as the SL guerrillas were in control in the Upper Huallaga Valley, they exacted an estimated 10 percent of the price of every kilo of coca paste.

---

[162] U.S. Department of State, Bureau for International Narcotics and Law Enforcement Affairs, *International Narcotics Control Strategy Report, 2001*, March 1, 2002.
[163] José E. Gonzales, "Guerrillas and Coca in the Upper Huallaga Valley," in David Scott Palmer, ed., *The Shining Path of Peru* (New York: St. Martin's Press, 1994), 123, citing Gustavo Gorriti and Raúl González.
[164] Simon Strong, *Shining Path: Terror and Revolution in Peru* (New York: Times Books/Random House, 1993), 98, 102.
[165] Ibid, 108-9.
[166] Ibid, 111.
[167] Ibid, 115.

The SL's annual revenue from charges levied against drug traffickers for use of SL-controlled airstrips in the Upper Huallaga Valley in the 1990s reportedly ranged from a low of $20 million to as much as $550 million.[168] The latter figure, however, is probably inflated.

Until production shifted to Colombia in the mid-1990s as a result of a disease that destroyed 30 percent of the coca plantations in Peru's upper Huallaga Valley, Peru was the world's largest coca producer. By the new millennium, Peru's drug business was generating an estimated $600 million a year. As Colombia's government stepped up the eradication of drug crops in 2001, the production of coca and poppies began to increase again in Peru. Even though 6,000 hectares were eradicated in Peru in 2001, Peru's coca crop in 2001 covered 34,000 hectares (84,000 acres), a reduction of only 500 acres from the previous year, according to official U.S. figures. The U.S. figure, however, is significantly lower than the 50,000 hectares estimated by Ricardo Vega Llona, Peru's drug czar, and the United Nations' preliminary estimate of about 44,000 hectares in 2000.[169] This increase has been helped by the rise in the farmers' price per kilo of coca of $3.50 in 2001, as compared with 40 cents in 1995.[170] In 2001 a total of 135 hectares of the relatively new opium poppy crop were eradicated, as compared with 26 in 2000.

As a result of the greatly reduced presence of the Peruvian Army in the drug areas as a result of budget cuts and international criticism of human rights abuses, a guerrilla revival in these areas was underway in 2001, with the 300-member Shining Path filling the vacuum left by the army. In addition, there have been rumors of FARC guerrillas infiltrating into Peru.

The SL's revival has been attributed to the group's new relationship with the FARC and Colombian drug traffickers. According to author Alberto Bolivar, the FARC and al Qaeda already operate with Shining Path in the drug business, trafficking in Peruvian poppy crops and heroin.[171]

In 2001, Peru had an estimated 34,600 hectares of coca, according to government estimates, down from 113,670 hectares six years ago. But analysts believe that coca cultivation could reach 70,000 hectares in 2002. Despite the growing popularity of poppy cultivation, coca leaf cultivation has been increasing in Peru's tropical regions.

---

[168] Cynthia McClintock. *Revolutionary Movements in Latin America: El Salvador's FMLN and Peru's Shining Path* (Washington: United States Institute of Peace Press, 1998), 72, 86.
[169] "Spectres Stir in Peru," *Economist* [London], February 16, 2002, 55.
[170] Ibid.

The Shining Path's Opium Production

The *International Narcotics Control Strategy Report, 2001* notes that Peruvian farmers are using Colombian poppy seeds provided by Colombian narcotraffickers, who are also supplying technical assistance and cash loans. By 2000 Shining Path guerrillas and the Colombian cartels had stepped up opium growing as a profitable sideline to the country's cocaine business. In contrast to cocaine, which sells for about $25,000 per kilo in the United States, heroin sells for $200,000 per kilogram in this country.[172] This fact means that heroin is much more profitable for Peruvian farmers, who make $800 to $1,200 for a liter of liquid extract, in contrast to the $40 paid for a bushel of coca. Moreover, poppies can be grown much more easily than coca. To cultivate poppy, a farmer has only to spread the seeds on damp ground and must wait only one year for the first harvest; there can be two harvests per year.

In 2000 Peruvian police destroyed 25 hectares of illegally grown opium poppies, but the figure rose to 1,150 hectares destroyed in 2001, along with an incremental increase in quantities of morphine and heroin.[173] The amount of captured opium poppies, however, was only a fraction of the total. Producing heroine, the final substance from poppy, is also much easier than producing cocaine hydrochloride. The refining process requires few chemical inputs, a fact that reduces the chances of being discovered by the police.[174]

Peruvian drug analysts believe that the Cali Cartel made a decision to develop new centers for producing the raw material for heroin as a result of increasing constraints on the producing market of Afghanistan and Pakistan. Peru is one of the chosen places because of its variety of climates and soils. According to *El Comercio*, Peruvian intelligence analysts have said that currently those who are training Peruvian growers to plant poppy are Colombian drug traffickers, who were in turn trained by Afghanis and Pakistanis with experience in both Asia and Colombia.[175] In addition, emissaries of the Carli Cartel have been bringing the seeds and inputs used in the plantings and in processing the poppy latex to convert it into heroin into Peru

[171] Alberto Bolivar, "The Return of the Shining Path," Foreign Policy Research Institute, April 5, 2002.
[172] Flor Huilca, *La República* (an independent center-leftist Lima daily, Internet Version-WWW), December 5, 2001, as translated in "Peru: 'Sudden Increase' in Opium Poppy Cultivation Seen," FBIS, LAP20011205000058, December 5, 2001.
[173] Paul Keller, "Peru Drugs Force Faces Upsurge in Opium Output," *Financial Times*, January 7, 2002.
[174] Huilca.
[175] *El Comercio* (Internet Version-WWW), November 5, 2001, as translated in "Peru: Increase in Opium Poppy Production Feared," FBIS, LAP20011105000079, November 5, 2001.

from Colombia via the Putumayo River and also from Ecuador, using the Napo and Pastaza Rivers. In addition, they are entering from Brazil through the border with Madre de Dios.

CONCLUDING POINTS

- The relationship between indigenous insurgent organizations in South America, on the one hand, and drug-trafficking cartels operating in the region, on the other, is a pragmatic, arm's-length relationship that is based on mutually beneficial advantages.

- For example, terrorist/guerrilla groups and drug-trafficking organizations in the region share similar methods of operation such as:

  —using similar methods to conceal profits, raise funds, and move or launder money, e.g., informal transfer systems, such as the Black Market Peso Exchange (BMPE), for general criminal purposes;

  —relying on bulk cash smuggling, multiple accounts, and front organizations to launder money;

  —using fraudulent documents, including passports and other identification documents, to travel worldwide;

  —using fraudulent customs declaration forms to smuggle drugs and weapons;

  —using networks of trusted couriers and contacts to conduct business;

  —using multiple cell phones and communications-security practices;

  —using illegal telephone exchanges equipped with PABX for connecting among telephone networks, thereby bypassing normal long-distance telephone calls and preventing satellite monitoring of overseas communications (see Triborder Region);

  —using online transfers and accounts that do not require disclosure of owners; relying on the same corrupt officials to gain greater access to fraudulent documents, including passports and customs papers; and

  —using similar clandestine methods or the same routes to smuggle drugs and weapons.

- Although this study does not suggest that the tightly knit Islamic fundamentalist cells can be infiltrated by agents, it does note that clandestine Argentine security agents were able to infiltrate mosques in the Triborder Region and an Islamic terrorist training camp and collect significant information as well as photos of terrorist leaders.

- Furthermore, given the numerous similarities between drug-trafficking terrorist and extremist groups and drug cartels in methods of operation and sharing of resources, a drug trafficker who is enticed by intelligence agencies to cooperate, such as by a promise of immunity from prosecution, could likely serve as a valuable source of information about a particular terrorist group.

- One of the most important means of combating terrorist networks appears to be through tracking and freezing the accounts or financing that make terrorism possible.[176]

- The war against al Qaeda provides a test case for expanding the counterterrorist war to other terrorist groups with transnational terrorist and criminal linkages. A *Jane's Intelligence Review* report suggests that current strategies to defeat al Qaeda by targeting bin Laden's top-tier command will not be effective. Instead, the strongest actions are currently being taken by U.S. intelligence agencies. "The key to disrupting, degrading and destroying al Qaeda," states the report, "lies in developing a multipronged, multidimensional and multinational strategy that targets the core and the penultimate leadership and the network's sources of finance and supplies."[177]

- Targeting a terrorist group's sources of finance and supplies increasingly means also targeting the drug cartels with which they do business, whether as a source of revenue or weapons.

- Targeting a terrorist group's key leadership may be even more essential than targeting the leadership of a drug cartel; whereas the latter's leadership can be easily and quickly replaced, the leadership of a terrorist or guerrilla group is not so easily replaced.

- Athough insufficient information was found to document the suspected drug-trafficking activities of Islamic fundamentalist groups operating in Latin America, the Islamic extremist groups operating in the region appear to derive large amounts of money from various illegal activities, such as extorting a "tax" on Muslim or Arab business people,

---

[176]See Sidney Weintraub, "Disrupting the Financing of Terrorism," *The Washington Quarterly*, 25, No. 1, Winter 2002.
[177] Rohan Gunaratna, Ed Blanche, Phil Hirschkorn, and Stefan Leader, "Osama bin Laden's Global 'al-Qaeda' Organisation," *Jane's Intelligence Review* [UK], August 13, 2001.

engaging in smuggling of contraband and arms and Black Market Peso Exchange (BMPE) operations, and so forth.

- The heavy involvement of the Colombian and Peruvian guerrilla/terrorist and paramilitary organizations in the drug trade is clear.

SELECTED BIBLIOGRAPHY

Bibes, Patricia. "Colombia: The Military and the Narco-Conflict," *Low Intensity Conflict & Law Enforcement*, 9, No. 1, Spring 2000, 32-48.

Bibes, Patricia. "Transnational Organized Crime and Terrorism: Colombia, a Case Study." *Journal of Contemporary Criminal Justice*, 17, No. 3, August 2001, 243-58.

Bodansky, Jossef. *Bin Laden: The Man Who Declared War on America*. Roseville, California: Prima Publishing/Random House, 2001.

Chalk, Peter. "Pakistan's Role in the Kashmir Insurgency," *Jane's Intelligence Review*, 13, No. 9, September 2001, 26-7.

Gheordunescu, Mircea. "Terrorism and Organized Crime: The Romanian Perspective," *Low Intensity Conflict & Law Enforcement*, 11, No. 4, Winter 1999, 24-9.

Gonzales, José E. "Guerrillas and Coca in the Upper Huallaga Valley." Pages 123-43 in David Scott Palmer, ed., *The Shining Path of Peru*. New York: St. Martin's Press, 1994.

Kay, Bruce H. "Violent Opportunities: The Rise and Fall of "King Coca" and Shining Path," *Journal of Interamerican Studies and World Affairs*, 41, No. 3, Fall 1999, 97-128.

Makarenko, Tamara. "Terrorism and Drug Trafficking Threaten Stability in Central Asia," *Jane's Intelligence Review*, 12, No. 11, November 2000, 28—30.

McClintock, Cynthia. *Revolutionary Movements in Latin America: El Salvador's FMLN and Peru's Shining Path*. Washington: United States Institute of Peace Press, 1998.

O'Balance, Edgar. Islamic Fundamentalist Terrorism, 1979-95: The Iranian Connection. New York: New York University Press, 1997.

Pardo, Rafael. "Colombia's Two-Front War," *Foreign Affairs*, 79, No. 4, July/August 2000, 64-73.

Rabasa, Angel, and Peter Chalk. *Colombian Labyrinth: The Synergy of Drugs and Insurgency and Its Implications for Regional Stability*. Santa Monica, California: Rand, 2001.

Reeve, Simon. *The New Jackals: Ramzi Yousef, Osama bin Laden and the Future of Terrorism*. Boston: Northeastern University Press, 1999.

Strong, Simon. *Shining Path: Terror and Revolution in Peru*. New York: Times Books/Random House, 1993.

Van de Velde, James R., "The Growth of Criminal Organizations and Insurgent Groups Abroad Due to International Drug Trafficking," *Low Intensity Conflict & Law Enforcement*, 5, No. 3, Winter 1996, 466-83.

Weintraub, Sidney. "Disrupting the Financing of Terrorism," *The Washington Quarterly*, 25, No. 1, Winter 2002, 53-60.

HIZBALLAH AND INTERNATIONAL NARCOTICS TRAFFICKING IN LEBANON AND SYRIA

Key Points

- Hizballah is a guerrilla group in southern Lebanon founded in the early 1980s to oppose Israel and its occupation of southern Lebanon, Gaza, and the West Bank of the Jordan River.

- Hizballah maintains that it is a resistance movement, not a terrorist or narcotics-driven organization. It claims to receive most of its funding from Iran and Syria.

- Major drug routes pass through Lebanon and Syria, and cannabis and some opium poppy are traditional crops in parts of Lebanon controlled by Hizballah and Syria.

- Hizballah does not appear to be engaged in local drug trafficking to any significant degree, although it is possible that it profits from a regional trade in cocaine.

Hizballah and the Narcotics Trade

Hizballah (also Hizbullah, Hezbollah, Hezballah), the "party of God," is a group of Shia militants known for anti-Western views and terrorist acts. It is based in Lebanon, particularly southern Lebanon and the Beka'a Valley. Hizballah's chief aim is the recovery of Arab land from Israeli occupation; it also believes in creation of an Islamic state in Lebanon.[178] Its current leader is Sheikh Hassan Nasrallah; the head of the party's security service is Imad Mugniyah, who has long-standing ties to Iranian intelligence agencies. Although its opponents label it a terrorist organization, Hizballah's leaders deny this. "Hizballah is known in the region as a resistance party. We were never a terrorist group," says Abdullah Qassir, Hizballah's representative in Lebanon's parliament.[179] Nonetheless, Hizballah is on the U.S. Department of State's list of Foreign Terrorist Organizations.

Although it has had contacts with larger worldwide terrorist groups such as al Qaeda, Hizballah for the most part has concentrated on its struggle with Israel rather than on activity in other regions of the world. Hizballah draws its recruits from the Lebanese/Palestinian population; it receives most of its financing, training, weapons, and organizational aid from Iran

---

[178] A brief overview of Hizballlah's beliefs and organization is in the profile of Hizballah, Council on Foreign Relations, <http://www.cfrterrorism.org>. See also Colin Shindler's review of *Hizbul'llah Politics and Religion* by Amal Saad-Ghorayeb, *The Jerusalem Post* [Jerusalem], February 8, 2002, 13B.

and Syria. It uses such assistance to sustain guerrilla warfare with Israel and social welfare programs among the local Shia population in Lebanon. There are indications that Hizballah is involved in narcotics trafficking and perhaps even in drug production, especially in the Beka'a Valley, but such activity appears to be minor and quite secondary to the struggle against Israel.

Well-established narcotics trafficking routes pass through Lebanon and Syria. One network originates in Iran and funnels heroin and opium westward from Afghanistan and points farther east via Lebanon and Syria and on to Mediterranean, European, and North African countries. Kurds, ethnic Arabs, and Baluchi nomads are among the most active groups involved in this trading network. One group of Arab and Iranian traders, known as the "Abadan drug ring," allegedly joined with Palestinians to help establish the Hizballah Party among the Shia of south Lebanon in the 1980s. Another narcotics network runs eastward from Turkey through Syria, Lebanon, and Jordan and provides mostly cocaine to the affluent societies of the Persian Gulf.[180]

Until at least the mid- or late 1990s, traffickers used five main routes to ship heroin from Lebanon—the Mediterranean, Romanian, Caribbean, Libyan, and Israeli routes.[181] The principal route, the Mediterranean route, utilized sea routes through the western Mediterranean Sea to make deliveries to Sicilian, Neapolitan, and Marseillaise mafia groups. On the Romanian route, heroin from Iran and Lebanon was shipped to the Romanian port of Constanta by sea, after which it was trucked through Hungary and turned over to Italian-, French-, and Sicilian-American mafia groups. The Caribbean and Libyan routes are extensions of the Colombian "Cali Cartel's" cocaine contraband network that supplies drugs to the United States and Europe. The Israeli route grew rapidly in and after the 1980s in step with various peace agreements between Israel and the Egyptians, Jordanians, and Palestinians. Both Arab and Jewish drug dealers participate in this commerce.

Aside from drug routes, drug cultivation is another aspect of the narcotics situation. Lebanese and Syrian farmers have traditionally raised cannabis, which is made into hashish, and some opium poppy, mostly for local consumption. Most Lebanese cannabis grows in the Beka'a

---

[179] Nicholas Blanford, "Freedom Fighters or Terrorists?" *Christian Science Monitor,* November 14, 2001, 6.
[180] On the east to west route, see Ivan Ivanov, "The International Illegal Drug Traffic and the former USSR," *Feliks' Publications* [Moscow], February 1, 1995, 1-81, FBIS Doc. ID FTS19970523002719; on the west to east route, see U.S. Dept. of State, "International Narcotics Control Strategy Report, 2001," entries for "Lebanon" and "Syria." <www.state.gov>
[181] Ivanov, 1-81.

Valley of Lebanon, an area controlled by Syria and a Hizballah stronghold. Beginning in the early 1990s, however, the Syrian and Lebanese governments joined international drug eradication campaigns and suppressed cannabis and opium poppy planting and drug processing laboratories within their borders. By 1999, this effort had almost completely eliminated both crops and had closed down many if not most processing facilities for heroin and other narcotics. Drug trafficking was similarly suppressed. The effort was so successful that in 1997 the United States removed Syria from its list of drug-producing nations.[182]

The role of Hizballah in drug production and trade in Lebanon is not clear from the research undertaken here, but it seems not to be of major dimensions. Most sources barely mention narcotics in their discussion of Hizballah or drug production, even when speaking of the Baka'a Valley. Rather than alleging Hizballah participation, one source paraphrases a Beka'a Valley farmer to the effect that Hizballah does not encourage cultivation of cannabis but tolerates it because otherwise local farmers would starve.[183] Still, it does appear that Hizballah operatives participate in some level of the narcotics trade, even if it is not particularly significant with respect to the narcotics trade beyond Lebanon.

A different perspective on this subject comes from Israeli sources, who allege that Hizballah, Lebanese traders, and the Syrians are deeply involved in drug production and trade. In a 1998 study, analysts with the International Policy Institute for Counterterrorism in Herzlia, Israel, acknowledged official efforts to reduce cultivation of cannabis and poppy in Lebanon during the 1990s, but they claimed that the Lebanese and Syrians had then turned to the production and marketing of heroin and cocaine in place of crop cultivation.[184]

According to these analysts, the raw materials for the production of cocaine and heroin flow into Lebanon along two central routes—the "Latin-American route" (Colombia, Peru, Brazil, etc.), along which Lebanese emigrants in these countries export hydrochloride used in the manufacture of cocaine, and the "Far East" route (Pakistan, Afghanistan, Iran, Turkey, and Syria), through which Lebanese traffickers import basic morphine, used to produce heroin. They allege that the heroin and cocaine manufactured in small laboratories spread out over the Beka'a

---

[182] U.S. Dept. of State, "Lebanon" and "Syria"; Hazim al-Amin, "Report on Cultivation of Cannabis in al-Biqa Valley," *Al Hayat* [London], October 2, 2001, 15; FBIS Doc ID GMP20011002000069.

[183] Hazim al-Amin, 15.

[184] International Policy Institute for Counterterrorism, "Removal of Syria, Lebanon From Drug List," Herzlia, Israel, April 24, 1998, FBIS Doc ID FTS19980428000915.

Valley are then marketed through a network of professional drug smugglers, Arab and Jewish, to the Middle East (including Israel), the Arab countries, and the West.[185]

Because the criminal networks involved in the production and marketing of drugs (as well as the forgery of U.S. and European currencies) are active in regions under Hizballah and Syrian military control, particularly the Beka'a Valley, the Israelis maintain that Hizballah and the Syrians must be intimately involved in narcotics trafficking. Aside from income that flows to Hizballah operatives and Syrian military officials, the analysts claim that profits from the drug trade "also significantly contribute to the economies of Syria and Lebanon and to the Hizballah as an organization (which needs large sums of money for its political-social activities in the Shiite community)."[186]

Israeli assertions about Hizballah's involvement in narcotics trafficking have continued to appear in the Israeli press. For example, in October 2001, a senior officer with the Israeli Defence Force's Northern Command asserted that "Hizballah controls the drugs market along the northern border. This organization's men . . . are supervising the drugs market and are closely controlling with whom to make the deals."[187]

Although the Israelis have a great deal of expertise when it comes to their neighbors, it should be remembered that they spare no effort to discredit Hizballah and the Syrians, with whom they have been locked in combat for decades. The assertions made above should be evaluated in this light.

The Israeli claims also need to be weighed against the findings of the U.S. Department of State in its *International Narcotics Control Strategy Report, 2001*, which found that "Lebanon is not a major illicit drug producing or drug-transit country, although it remains a country of concern to the U.S."[188] Despite a resurgence in cannabis cultivation since 2000, cannabis and opium poppy production remain subdued. "There is no significant illicit drug refining in Lebanon; such activity has practically disappeared due to vigilance of the Syrian and Lebanese governments."[189] And finally, "Lebanon is not a major transit country for illicit drug traffickers,

---

[185] International Policy Institute for Counterterrorism.
[186] International Policy Institute for Counterterrorism.
[187] Eytan Glickman, "Hizballah Controls Drugs Market in the North," *Yedi'ot Aharonot* [Tel Aviv], October 29, 2001, 14; FBIS Doc ID GMP20011029000106.
[188] U.S. Dept. of State, "Lebanon."
[189] U.S. Dept. of State, "Lebanon."

and most trafficking is done by 'amateurs' rather than major drug networks. Marijuana and opium derivatives are trafficked to a modest extent in the region . . . ."[190]

The State Department report notes continued improvement in the narcotics situation in Syria as well, although a significant amount of drugs, including cocaine, transits the country, mostly bound for Persian Gulf states.[191] Yet another source refines the narcotics picture by distinguishing between drug trafficking, allegedly conducted by Syrian military and other officials, and drug cultivation, which profits Lebanese farmers and groups such as Hizballah.[192] As cannabis and opium poppy production dropped through the 1990s, apparently with Hizballah's concurrence, so, too, did income from these crops that reportedly went to farmers and possibly Hizballah. The recent increase in Lebanese cannabis production has been attributed to relaxed enforcement and lack of substitute crops at a time of economic difficulty for Lebanese farmers.

CONCLUDING POINTS

- Hizballah may be involved in the narcotics trade in Lebanon and Syria, but on the basis of the present research effort, that involvement appears to be local and small-scale.

- Hizballah maintains that its paramount concern is opposition to Israel and its occupation of Arab land. It apparently receives most of its funding from Syria and Iran in order to carry out its mission, and little, if anything, from trade in narcotics.

- Cocaine from South America flows through Lebanese and Syrian hands. It is possible that Hizballah operatives are involved in cocaine trafficking, although this research effort uncovered no reports of such activity.

- Further research might indicate that Hizballah is involved to a significant degree in cocaine and general drug trafficking in the eastern Mediterranean. Israeli sources certainly maintain that this is the case, and even the U.S. Department of State's narcotics report does not categorically rule out such a possibility.

---

[190] U.S. Dept. of State, "Lebanon."
[191] U.S. Dept. of State, "Syria."
[192] Hillary Mann, "Removing Syria From the Narcotics List—A Signal to Damascus?" *Policywatch*, No. 277, November 10, 1997. <http://www.washingtoninstitute.org>

DRUG-FUNDED TERRORIST/EXTREMIST GROUPS IN ALBANIA AND THE BALKANS

Key Points

- In early 2002, the preponderance of potential guerrilla and terrorist activity in the areas in and around Albania was confined to a few splinter groups located in northwestern Macedonia and fed by personnel and equipment from Kosovo and Albania. The Kosovo Liberation Army (KLA) and its most significant offshoots have nominally disarmed, leaving some of their personnel and weaponry unaccounted for.

- Regional intelligence agencies in the Balkans have identified a link between current guerrilla/terrorist groups and the large amount of trafficking in narcotics, arms, and people that is indigenous to the region. Specific activities and levels have not been documented, however.

- Regional trafficking in the Balkans and the Adriatic is likely to remain at a high level, thus presenting an ongoing opportunity for guerrilla/terrorist groups to participate. That trend is promoted by the increased inter-group cooperation and sophistication that has been noted in recent years in the Balkan and Adriatic regions.

Terrorist/Extremist Groups and Narcotics

The Kosovo Liberation Army (KLA, also known by its Albanian-derived acronym UCK) nominally was converted into a territorial security organization, called the Kosovo Protection Corps, after NATO troops occupied Kosovo in 1999. However, far from all of the KLA's personnel and weapons were transferred into the new organization. Members of the protection corps also reportedly have engaged in illegal activities, taking advantage of their newly legitimate position. Officials of the corps have expressed dissatisfaction that the force is controlled by NATO rather than by the Kosovo government.[193]

Smaller terrorist organizations calling themselves liberation groups have emerged from the former KLA in the years since 1999. Many of an estimated 20,000 former fighters that were assigned to the Protection Corps formed small militia groups that are active mainly in the U.S. occupation zone of Kosovo. These groups have received weapons and money from the KLA's still active fund-raising organization. Their umbrella organization was the Liberation Army of

Presevo, Medvedja, and Bujanovac (PMBLA, UCPMB in Albanian). The region that includes those three districts along Serbia's southwestern border with Kosovo remained a hotbed of rebel activity even after the UCPMB officially ended armed resistance in May 2001.[194] In southern Kosovo, the Liberation Army of Eastern Kosovo and the National Liberation Army of Western Kosovo, formed from the UCPMB, have continued to exert pressure for that part of southern Serbia, which has a large Albanian population, to be added to Kosovo.

The Albanian National Army (Albanian initialism AKSh), a successor group to the National Liberation Army (NLA, another group that nominally ended hostilities in 2001) has continued insurgency in northern Macedonia on behalf of the rights of the Albanian minority in that country.[195] During their active existence, both the UCPMB and the NLA were accused of firing on civilian population centers and committing terrorist acts in their respective regions, as well as conducting armed attacks against government forces in Serbia and Macedonia.[196] Those groups were nominally disarmed under the terms of the August 2001 peace settlement. In early 2002, a new splinter group calling itself the True National Liberation Army began threatening to resume armed conflict unless the government of Macedonia increased constitutional protections for the Albanian minority.[197] In March 2002, Macedonian security authorities reported that 150 members of the Kosovo Protection Corps had crossed the border into Macedonia to join the AKSh and were recruiting in the Kumanovo region.[198] However, the consensus of reports in March 2002 was that the extremist AKSh remained isolated and that the prospects of renewed terrorism in northern Macedonia had been significantly reduced by events of the past year. Rivalry between the AKSh and remaining NLA forces under Ali Ahmeti was exposed in late March 2002, when AKSh forces attacked Ahmeti's headquarters near the north Albanian city of

---

[193] "Kosovo Leader Dissatisfied with Status," ONASA News Agency report, February 6, 2002.

[194] "Shefket Musliu, Commander of the UCPMB, Turns Himself In," Task Force Falcon Press Release No. 92-01, May 26, 2001. <http://www.tffalcon.hqusareur.army.mil>

[195] "FYROM Interior Ministry: 'Small' Amount of Arms Entering from Kosovo, Albania," MIA report, January 29, 2002 (FBIS Document EUP20020129000430).

[196] United States Department of State, Office of the Coordinator for Counterterrorism, *Patterns of Global Terrorism 2000.* <http://www.milnet.com/milnet/state/2000/europaoverview>

[197] Christian Jennings, "Fear over Islamic Terror Groups Using Macedonia as Base," *The Scotsman*, March 4, 2002, 9.

[198] Tanjug News Agency [Belgrade], "Macedonian Sources Say 150 Former Kosovo Rebels Joined ANA Ranks," March 30, 2002.

Tetovo.[199] Ahmeti subsequently requested that the Kosovo Protection Corps prevent former KLA members from crossing into Macedonia and joining the AKSh.[200]

According to a February 2002 report in the *Daily Telegraph* and the Macedonian daily *Nova Makedonija*, Western police records and United Nations reports confirm that the leaders of the AKSh and the NLA are involved in large-scale smuggling of weapons, human beings, narcotics, and other goods. Money from those transactions is used to finance terrorist activities in Macedonia and Kosovo. Narcotics, reportedly the most important of the smuggled items, are moved through what is known as the Balkan Drug Route, which begins in Afghanistan and passes through Turkey, Bulgaria, Macedonia, Albania, and Italy to reach markets in Western Europe. An alternate route goes from Afghanistan into Western Europe via Turkey, Bulgaria, Serbia, and Slovenia. Primary locations for the exchange of drugs for guns are Kumanovo and Skopje (both in northern Macedonia), which are points along the Balkan route to which weapons are smuggled. From those cities, weapons move into Kosovo.[201]

In September 2001, the Canadian Centre for Peace in the Balkans reported that Osama bin Laden was channeling profits from the sale of narcotics arriving in Western Europe via the Balkan Route to local governments and political parties, with the goal of gaining influence in Albania or Macedonia or both. The report theorized that Macedonia presents an ideal target because of its large Albanian minority (about one in three Macedonians is an ethnic Albanian) and its strategic position between east and west, along the new pipeline proposed between Burgas (Bulgaria) and Drac (Albania).[202]

In the same period, the *Washington Times* reported that bin Laden was the "biggest financial supporter" of the NLA, which has received $6 to $7 million from that source to supplement its narcotics income in supporting terrorist activities. In January 2001, the Stratfor intelligence organization reported that bin Laden had contributed and trained fighters for the KLA, citing the strategic importance of this link for the operation of his terrorist network in Europe. That report quoted the Albanian intelligence service as calling Albania the most

---

[199] "FYROM Intelligence Sources Claim Former TMK Members Joined ANA Ranks," Tanjug (Press Agency of Yugoslavia) report, March 30, 2002 (FBIS Document EUP20020330000131).
[200] Magdalena Andonovska, "Ali Ahmeti in Kosovo for Consultations with Agim Ceku!?" *Nova Makedonija*, March 29, 2002, 3 (FBIS Document EUP20020329000127).
[201] "Macedonian Government Confirms Ethnic Albanians Buying Arms from Drug Funds," *Nova Makedonija* [Skopje], February 20, 2002.
[202] "Dnevnik Daily Views Ties between Bin-Ladin, NLA," Macedonian Press Agency report, September 20, 2001.

important transit point for Islamic militants into Europe. In 1999 and 2000, Albania arrested ten individuals identified as Islamic terrorists.[203]

A February 2002 report in the *Herald* of Glasgow noted that al Qaeda had acted as a middleman in the movement of heroin from warehouses in Afghanistan via Chechen mafia conduits and into the Balkan narcotics pipeline. (The Taliban had prohibited the growing of poppies but had not confiscated the large stores of heroin already existing, and in fact profited from the heroin trade by taxing growers and dealers.) Al Qaeda took a percentage of the drug profits for this service.[204] Between 1996 and 1998, the volume of drugs confiscated by Italian police from Albanian dealers in Italy rose from 5,500 kilograms to 23,000 kilograms.[205]

According to a February 2002 report, former KLA guerrillas and Albanian liberation extremists have used profits from their participation in Taliban-sponsored narcotics smuggling to re-arm themselves after the disarmaments that occurred from 1999 to 2001. The new arms, estimated to be worth about $4 million, include SA-18 and SA-7 surface-to-air missiles capable of bringing down Macedonian helicopters.[206] According to a subsequent report, "the weapons were paid for by Albanian criminals with the proceeds of selling Afghan heroin on the streets of a dozen European capitals."[207]

Beginning in the 1990s, the "official" network of organized crime in Albania has grown and become more sophisticated. In a January 2001 report, British-based criminologist Vicenzo Ruggiero said, "joint ventures between southern Italian organized crime and groups operating in Albania are frequent, and such partnerships are imposed by local criminal entrepreneurs who expect to be given a percentage of the profits earned by their Albanian counterparts." According to Italian prosecutor Piero Luigi Vigna, Albanian groups have found a specific niche in the growing multinational organized crime network: "Albanian criminal groups fulfill the functions of a kind of service agency, establishing, for the management of clandestine immigration toward [sic] Italy, ties with the Chinese mafia and with its Turkish and Russian counterparts." Thus cooperative agreements and the development of specific roles appear to be replacing traditional

---

[203] "Dnevnik Daily Views Ties between Bin-Ladin, NLA."
[204] Ian Bruce, "U.S. Aid Goes Ahead despite Failure to Curb Poppy Crop," *The Herald* [Glasgow], February 27, 2002.
[205] Frank Viviano, "New Face of Mafia in Sicily: High-Tech Transformation with Global Tentacles," *San Francisco Chronicle*, January 8, 2001. <http://AmericanMafia.com/news>
[206] Bruce Garvey, "U.S. Backed Albanian Rebels with al Qaeda Links, Book Says: Author Predicts Renewed Balkan War" [book review of *Diary of an Uncivil War* by Scott Taylor], *Ottawa Citizen*, February 22, 2002.
[207] Jennings.

bloody territorial rivalries between crime groups from various nations (most importantly for the Balkan and Adriatic regions, groups from Albania and Italy).[208]

Trafficking in human beings is an expanding activity for this international network. According to the International Organisation for Migration, the Balkans is a major route (and source) for trafficking in women and children for sexual exploitation. The organization characterizes such trafficking as "the fastest-growing crime in the Balkans."[209] Albania's geographical position and its chaotic political situation mean that it plays an important role in such trade. One factor in the expansion of this commerce has been the presence in the Balkans of foreign soldiers, who in 2000 accounted for 80 percent of the profits of brothels in Kosovo and Bosnia.[210] Many women are moved across the Albanian border into the coastal tourist areas of Greece. Reportedly, the young women of entire villages in Albania, Bulgaria, Moldova, and Romania have been forcibly moved into this system, many with the promise of reaching Western Europe. Corrupt police in Albania have aided this practice, even escorting women through the country.[211] The port of Vlore, characterized as "lawless" in 2001, has been the home port of a large fleet of boats that have smuggled hundreds of thousands of immigrants and tons of drugs across the Adriatic Sea into Italy, and thence into the rest of Western Europe.[212]

A March 2002 report of the Ministry of Interior of Macedonia confirmed that terrorist groups such as the AKSh are engaged in human trafficking as well as narcotics and weapons smuggling.[213] There is no documentation of specific cooperation in these activities between the terrorist groups and Albanian organized crime groups. However, the new atmosphere of cooperation among criminal groups and the need for international markets for all types of trafficking makes a strong circumstantial case for at least some degree of mutual assistance.

---

[208] Viviano, "New Mafias Go Global High-Tech Trade in Humans, Drugs," *San Francisco Chronicle*, January 7, 2001, and "New Face of Mafia in Sicily: High-Tech Transformation with Global Tentacles."

[209] Agence France Press, "Sex-Slave Trade Flourishes in the Balkans," January 15, 2002.

[210] "Sex-Slave Trade Flourishes in the Balkans," Agence France Press report, January 15, 2002.

[211] Helena Smith, "Trade in Sex Rocks Greece," *Sunday Herald Sun* [London], February 10, 2002, and Agence France Press, "Sex-Slave Trade Flourishes in the Balkans."

[212] Viviano, "New Mafias Go Global High-Tech Trade in Humans, Drugs," and "New Face of Mafia in Sicily: High-Tech Transformation with Global Tentacles."

[213] "Macedonian Government Confirms Ethnic Albanians Buying Arms from Drug Funds."

Money Laundering and Business Links

In December 2001, Albanian authorities announced discovery of a major instance of terrorist support money being concealed behind the facade of a legitimate business operating in Albania. Yasin al-Qadi (variant spellings of the last name are Kadi and Kadiu), the Saudi Arabian head of a company called Karavan Construction, has been accused of using a twin-tower construction project being built by that company in Tirana to launder money for al Qaeda. Karavan owns 34 percent of the building project; according to Albanian authorities, the other owners, all Albanian, are not under suspicion of having terrorist ties.[214] Al-Qadi also is the head of a Saudi-based charity foundation, Muwafaq (Blessed Relief), which is suspected of channeling the millions of dollars that it receives from Saudi businessmen to al Qaeda. Al-Qadi is on the list of individuals suspected of having terrorist connections, released by the United States in October 2001.[215] He has remained in Saudi Arabia since the investigation was announced. No connection has been made between al-Qadi and organized crime organizations in Albania.

The Albanian government has frozen the assets of Karavan in two banks in Albania, the International Trade Bank of Malaysia and the Arab-Albanian-Islamic Bank, as well as the buildings under construction. However, the governor of the State Bank of Albania has speculated that other banks in Albania also are servicing accounts and transactions for the terrorist organization.[216] Al-Qadi also has accounts in nine other banks in Albania: the Savings Bank of Albania, the Italian-Albanian Bank, the Dardania Bank, the Tirana Bank, the Fefad Bank, the First Investment Bank, the Alfa Credit Bank, the Greek National Bank, and the American Bank of Albania. Reportedly, in the last five years about $2.3 million passed through al-Qadi's account in the former bank, and $500,000 passed through his account in the latter.[217] Authorities were alerted by the large size of transactions in those accounts and by the concealment of financial transaction records by subsidiary firms of Karavan. Nine instances of money laundering were reported by banks, involving 16 individuals, all of whom were under investigation in

---

[214] "Albania Freezes Saudi Businessman's Assets and Seeks His Arrest; Allegedly Linked to bin Laden," Financial Times Information Global News Wire report, February 5, 2002.

[215] Merita Dhimgjoka, "Assets of Saudi Suspected of Laundering Money for al-Qaida Frozen in Albania," Associated Press Worldstream, January 22, 2002.

[216] Alban Bala, "Albania: Officials Crack Down on Terror Suspects," Radio Free Europe/Radio Liberty report, January 25, 2002. <http://www.rferl.org/nca/features>

[217] "Arab of Tirana Towers Owns Accounts in 11 Banks in Albania," Gazeta Shqiptare [Tirana], January 25, 2002 (FBIS Document EUP20020125000442).

January 2002.[218] The accounts in the two named banks of several other Arab companies—based in Algeria, Egypt, Jordan, and Saudi Arabia—also have been frozen. Primary responsibility for investigating this situation belongs to the Ministry of Finance, which has moved cautiously to this point.

Other possible business ties with al Qaeda have surfaced in recent months in Albania. In January 2002, the Italian press reported that a $100 million contract to build a highway across Albania from the port of Durres to Pogradec in Macedonia had been won by a consortium that includes firms from Italy, Macedonia, and Turkey. The fourth member of the consortium is the Kuwaiti-based Kharafi Group, which intelligence services suspect is owned by companies at least partly controlled by Osama bin Laden. Kharafi also built the Chateau Linza Hotel east of Tirana near a location where bin Laden reportedly met with Islamic groups, and Kharafi is under contract for a $20-million harbor improvement project in Durres. That project is critical for Albania because Durres is its largest port.[219]

Prior to the al-Qadi case, Albanian authorities had denied consistently the existence of any parts of a terrorist network in their country. As part of the new campaign to remove suspicion that Albania is a base for terrorist groups, as of late January 2002, the government of Prime Minister Ilir Meta had deported five individuals on the general charge of threatening Albania's relations with other countries. The action was presumably based on the individuals' perceived link with terrorist activities. Another 223 individuals have been asked to leave because they were found to have invalid residency permits.[220] However, the Meta government was replaced in late February by one formed by a new prime minister, Pandeli Majko of the opposition Socialist Party. The effect of this change on Meta's National Action Plan Against Terrorism was not immediately known.

CONCLUDING POINTS

- In the past year, progress has been made in pacifying the regions where Albanian terrorist organizations were most active. The disarmament of several groups (even considering

---

[218] Altin Kreka, "Meta at Assembly: How al-Qu'aida Operated in Albania," *Gazeta Shqiptare* [Tirana], January 22, 2002 (FBIS Document EUP20020122000087).
[219] Vicenzo Tessendori, "The Opportunities that Have Slipped Through the Italians' Fingers in Albania," *La Stampa* [Turin], January 17, 2002 (FBIS Document EUP20020117000015).
[220] Bala.

that some members have remained at large and armed) reduces at least the scale of future guerrilla and terrorist activity in southern Serbia and northern Macedonia.

- Splinter groups such as the Albanian National Army are likely to remain beyond the control of international and domestic authorities in Macedonia; such groups will be motivated by unresolved territorial and political demands and supported by participation in the ongoing, globalized trafficking operations of the region.

SELECTED BIBLIOGRAPHY

Cilluffo, Frank J., and George Salmoiraghi. "And the Winner Is....the Albanian Mafia," *The Washington Quarterly*, 22, No. 4, Autumn 1999, 21-25.

Loza, Tihomir. "The KLA Cleansed," *The Nation*, May 17, 1999, 5-6.

Raufer, Xavier, and Stephen Quere. *La Mafia Albanaise, une Ménace pour l'Europe: Comment Est Née cette Superpuissance Criminelle Balkanique* (The Albanian Mafia, a Threat to Europe: How This Balkan Criminal Superpower Came to Be). Lausanne: Favre, 2000.

DRUG-FUNDED TERRORIST/EXTREMIST GROUPS IN CENTRAL ASIA

Key Points

- In Central Asia, the Islamic Movement of Uzbekistan (IMU) is the most widespread and best-financed terrorist group. It seeks to use its excellent connections with the Taliban and al Qaeda to topple the Karimov regime in Uzbekistan and establish a wider Islamic state in Central Asia.

- The IMU is known to rely heavily on narcotics trafficking over a number of Central Asian routes to support its military, political, and propaganda activities. That trafficking is based on moving heroin from Afghanistan through Tajikistan, Uzbekistan, and Kyrgyzstan, into Russia, and then into Western Europe.

- Markets and processing capacity for this commerce are expanding into new parts of Central Asia, and the IMU is able to adjust its military and trafficking activities to respond to interdiction in given areas. Military losses in Afghanistan are not likely to have a long-term effect.

- The Hizb-ut-Tahrir (HT) is a fundamentalist Islamic group whose membership in Uzbekistan, Kyrgyzstan, and Tajikistan is expanding rapidly. To this point, HT has relied on peaceful means to propagate its central idea of Islamic governance throughout Central Asia.

- HT's decentralized structure conceals its activities very effectively. Although HT has funded its widespread educational and propaganda network primarily from overseas contributions, individual cells may be involved in narcotics trafficking.

- HT's expanding appeal among the poor provides a strong base for potential terrorist activity, and ongoing repression in Kyrgyzstan and Uzbekistan may drive at least some parts of the organization to respond violently.

The Islamic Movement of Uzbekistan (IMU)

Two major Islamic groups with extreme political programs have surfaced in Central Asia in the past ten years. The first, the Islamic Movement of Uzbekistan (IMU), was founded in 1998 by the charismatic Uzbek guerrilla fighter Juma Namangani (original name Jumaboy Hojiyev) and another Uzbek, Tohir Yuldeshev, who became the political leader of the organization. The proximate goal of the group was to overthrow the repressive regime of President Islam Karimov

89

of Uzbekistan, who had imprisoned many members of Islamic groups that were predecessors to the IMU.[221] According to regional expert Ahmed Rashid, Namangani's group has a close relationship with al Qaeda: "In the IMU, [al Qaeda leader Osama] bin Laden cultivated a cultlike group that could act as a bridge to Afghanistan's landlocked, mountainous neighbors—neighbors who were striking deals with American oil and gas companies and looking increasingly to Washington for assistance." In the past two years, Namangani received an estimated $35 million from al Qaeda[222] (including $20 million given personally by bin Laden) to buy arms and equipment for his organization.[223] According to Rashid, bin Laden also considered Central Asia as a prime source of new recruits to his cause, and the IMU as a prime instrument in the recruitment process.

An avowedly terrorist organization, the IMU has been especially active in areas adjacent to the Fergana Valley, which is the economic and natural resource center of Central Asia. The IMU aims to capture that critical region and establish an Islamic caliphate that would eventually expand to rule all of Central Asia. In 1999 and 2000, Fergana, which includes territory of Uzbekistan, Tajikistan, and Kyrgyzstan, was the scene of terrorist actions that included the kidnapping of Japanese, Kyrgyz, and American citizens in Kyrgyzstan. In the same period, IMU fighters were training and recruiting with Taliban forces in Afghanistan, where IMU leaders had established close connections. Before September 11, the IMU was an active participant in the Taliban's struggle to gain full control of Afghanistan against resistance forces in the northeast of that country. Under Namangani's command, an IMU force reportedly 3,000 to 5,000 strong fought beside the Taliban regime against U.S. and Afghan forces in the campaign of late 2001.[224] Some IMU forces reportedly remained with holdout Taliban forces in eastern Afghanistan as late as February 2002.[225] Namangani's reported death in the Afghan fighting had not been confirmed as of April 2002.[226] His most likely place of refuge at that point was said to be eastern Iran.

---

[221] Tom Walker, "Passions Running at Their Height," review of Ahmed Rashid's *Jihad*, *Sunday Times* [London], February 3, 2002.
[222] Ahmed Rashid, "Why Militant Islamicists in Central Asia Aren't Going to Go Away," *The New Yorker*, January 14, 2002.
[223] Jonathon Curiel, "From the Cauldron's Edge: *Taliban* Author Offers Rare Insight into Troubled Territories," review of Ahmed Rashid's *Jihad*, *San Francisco Chronicle Sunday Review*, March 3, 2002, 1.
[224] Armen Khanbabyan, "To the Evident Indifference of Moscow," *Nezavisimaya Gazeta* [Moscow], February 6, 2002, 5.
[225] Todd Zeranski, "Al Qaeda Ally in Central Asia Poses Lingering Threat, *Bloomberg News*, March 12, 2002.
[226] "Wanted Uzbek Islamic Leader May Be Still Alive—Kazakh Paper."

In 1999 stringent security procedures by the Uzbek armed forces, together with pressure from the Tajikistan government to vacate bases in that country, caused the IMU to begin a quiet infiltration into Kyrgyzstan.[227] Kyrgyzstan also is a primary IMU target because it is the only Central Asian country to allow the activity of Christian missionaries.[228] In 2001 the IMU mounted guerrilla attacks in southwestern Kyrgyzstan from sleeper cells already in that country, rather than by moving fighters across the border from Tajikistan as it had in the attacks of 1999 and 2000. This new stratagem is significant because it reduced pressure on the IMU from the Tajikistan government and confirmed a permanent IMU presence in Kyrgyzstan.[229] Establishment of a beachhead in Kyrgyzstan has been facilitated by inept and uncoordinated border controls in the region where Kyrgyzstan, Tajikistan, and Uzbekistan meet. According to Rashid, the mutual distrust of these three states have for each other and Uzbekistan's unilateral mining of its portion of the border have increased the incidence of smuggling activity, which supports the IMU. It also has disrupted the trans-border trade that is the foundation of the region's economy, thus exacerbating the conditions that foster extremist recruitment.[230]

Narcotics Activity in Central Asia

Besides money from bin Laden and sources in Saudi Arabia, IMU funding is known to rely heavily on narcotics trafficking, using connections that Namangani developed in Afghanistan and Tajikistan during his pre-IMU participation in the Tajik civil war (1992-97). Regional expert Frederick Starr has characterized the relationships that have developed as a "potent amalgam of personal vendetta, Islamism, drugs, geopolitics, and terrorism."[231] Both before and after the founding of the IMU in 1998, Namangani developed enclaves stretching from Tavildara west of Dushanbe to the Sukh and Vorukh enclaves, which are tiny territorial islands and hotbeds of radical Islam located in far southwestern Kyrgyzstan, just south of the Fergana Valley. Those enclaves also are centers of hostility among the three states because they belong respectively to Uzbekistan and Tajikistan. Such hostility, which has been fostered especially by Karimov's intransigence on a number of regional issues, enables the IMU to play

---

[227] Svante E. Cornell and Regine A. Spector, "Central Asia: More than Islamic Extremists," *The Washington Quarterly*, 25, No. 1, 2002.
[228] Ahmed Rashid, *Jihad: The Rise of Militant Islam in Central Asia* (New Haven and London: Yale University Press, 2002), 130.
[229] Rashid, *Jihad*, 181-82.
[230] Rashid, *Jihad,* 161.

one side against the other, gain influence with corrupt officials on all sides, and stir anti-government resistance among the regional populations.[232]

State corruption has played a role in the IMU's success. Based on its role in the civil war, the IMU now has "contacts in Tajikistan's highest echelons of power,"[233] which are useful in protecting narcotics routes. The Tajik government still does not exercise significant control outside the immediate area of Dushanbe, relying heavily on Russian troops and border guards.

According to a 2002 analysis, more than half of Afghanistan's opium exports move through Turkmenistan and Tajikistan. Between 1998 and 1999, a critical point at which the IMU was using its network of militants and its contacts with Chechen guerrillas to expand its narcotics sales, the production of opium in Afghanistan nearly doubled. The IMU is known to control opium movement through these Central Asian routes, including as much as 70 percent of the opium trade entering Kyrgyzstan. With constriction of the narcotics route from Uzbekistan's border with Afghanistan across Uzbekistan through Bukhara and Urgench to Nukus in the western province of Karakalpakstan and thence into Kazakhstan and Russia, the volume of narcotics traffic into Kyrgyzstan increased significantly after 1999.[234]

In 2001 the IMU reportedly set up heroin refining laboratories in Tajikistan. In July of that year, Russian border guards seized 2.4 tons of raw opium on the Afghanistan-Tajikistan border, a sign that opium was being processed in Tajikistan.[235] The movement of narcotics through Tajikistan is facilitated by paying off Tajik officials and members of the Russian military. Reportedly, military vehicles returning to Moscow from supply missions in Central Asia are used to transport narcotics to that major center of international trafficking.[236]

Several factors have promoted the narcotics trade in Central Asia since the breakup of the Soviet Union: a common regional language; proximity to two of the three largest sources of narcotics in the world, the Golden Triangle of Southeast Asia and the Golden Crescent in Afghanistan and Pakistan; porous border controls exacerbated by rugged terrain; the central geographic position of conflict-wracked Tajikistan; and stricken economies throughout the

---

[231] Zeranski.
[232] Rashid, *Jihad,* 161.
[233] Cornell and Spector.
[234] V. Januzakov, chief of national security force of Kyrgyzstan, speech to international forum "Strategy for Combating Terrorism: Political-Legal Mechanisms," Bishkek, October 19, 2001 (FBIS Document CEP2001109000271).
[235] Rashid, *Jihad,* 165-66.
[236] Cornell and Spector.

region that make officials and ordinary citizens easily amenable to bribes.[237] The drug trade from Afghanistan through Tajikistan, Uzbekistan, and Kyrgyzstan already was prospering long before the IMU was founded.[238] Government repression of Islamic opposition groups in all five Central Asian republics has promoted an extremist religious-political underworld that has expanded those networks for its own purposes. In 2000 a kilogram of raw opium costing $50 in Afghanistan cost $10,000 in Moscow, and a kilogram of heroin made from that opium brought as much as $200,000 in New York and London.[239]

In recent years, significant changes have occurred in the structure of narcotics routes involving Central Asia. Russia has changed from an end-point of Central Asian narcotics routes to another trans-shipment point, mainly through Moscow and St. Petersburg. Another change is that Central Asian republics now are becoming suppliers of narcotics. Tajikistan and Kyrgyzstan, once only trans-shipment regions for Asian heroin, now also grow significant amounts of poppies. Kyrgyzstan's annual heroin output potential is estimated at 180 to 220 tons. Illegal laboratories in Kyrgyzstan also use indigenous ephedra to produce an estimated 500 tons of ephedrine, which can be used in amphetamines. The Chu Valley, which extends across northern Kyrgyzstan and southern Kazakhstan, yields a very large crop of marijuana. That region is adjacent to the metropolitan centers of Bishkek and Almaty. Narcotics addiction is rising within the Central Asian republics as well,[240] providing additional markets—although obviously higher profits come from exports to the West.

The prospect of substantial profits (even though local participants gain a very small percentage of the total) drives pragmatic adjustments of routes and markets when authorities are able to block traffic in a given area. Experts attribute the substantial yearly increase in the volume of narcotics seized by authorities to an increase in traffic rather than to an improvement of interdiction techniques.[241] In 1999 Kyrgyz authorities effectively blocked one major route, passing from Afghanistan through Khorog on Tajikistan's border with Afghanistan, north across the Pamir Mountains to the major Kyrgyz population center of Osh in the Fergana Valley. Since

---

[237] Martha Brill Olcott and Natalia Udalova, "Drug Trafficking on the Great Silk Road: The Security Environment in Central Asia," Carnegie Endowment for International Peace, *Working Papers*, No. 11, 2000, 14.

[238] Olcott and Udalova, 12.

[239] Estimates by Ministry of Interior of Russian Federation and United Nations Drug Control Programme, cited in Olcott and Udalova.

[240] "Afghan Political Revival Seen Letting Central Asia Drugs Traffic Flourish," *Nezavisimaya Gazeta* [Moscow], February 4, 2002.

[241] Olcott and Udalova.

that time, the volume of smuggling has not decreased; rather, a wider variety of routes has been used.[242]

Tajikistan's vast, mountainous eastern province of Gorno-Badakhshan, which is sparsely populated, destitute, and virtually roadless,[243] continues to provide ideal conditions for the movement of narcotics, despite intensified efforts by Russian forces to monitor such activities. The province's southern border is defined by mountainous northeastern Afghanistan. A major route between Tajikistan and southern Russia is the railroad between Dushanbe and Astrakhan, which is known as the "drug train." In 2001 a shipment of 120 kilograms (264 pounds) of heroin was discovered in a passenger car in Astrakhan. Small amounts of heroin are carried on the same route by many individual couriers.[244] In early 2002, the typical size of heroin shipments intercepted at the Afghanistan-Tajikistan border was 10 to 20 kilograms.[245]

According to regional expert Martha Brill Olcott, the IMU's manpower base was significantly scattered and reduced by the results of the Afghan conflict.[246] For that reason, the organization's resumption of its campaign to gain control of the Fergana Valley in 2002 is considered doubtful. Although the long-term effect of the Afghan campaign on the IMU is unknown, the organization has lost its military bases and Taliban support in Afghanistan for the foreseeable future. However, the IMU reportedly still was recruiting new members, receiving aid from al Qaeda, and fanning anti-American sentiment in February of 2002. Kyrgyzstan continued to be an important bastion of the group.[247] Both the U.S. presence in Central Asia and the ongoing economic crisis in the Fergana region contributed to the success of IMU's recruiting campaigns.

The effect of military losses on the group's narcotics trade is unknown. In early 2002, Russian authorities reported an increased flow of narcotics across the Afghanistan-Tajikistan border.[248] Ahmed Rashid asserts that the political arm of the IMU under Yuldashev has been a separate branch of the organization and therefore has survived the military losses incurred in

---

[242] Cornell and Spector.

[243] Olcott and Udalova.

[244] David Stern, "The Tajikistan Trail: Young Men Risk Death on Drugs Train to Europe," *Financial Times*, January 10, 2002, 10.

[245] "Tajik Drug Trade Thriving in Northern Afghanistan and Tajikistan," *Monitor*, v. 8, No. 15, January 22, 2002.

[246] Interview, *The News Hour*, March 12, 2002.

[247] "Banned Islamic Movement Still 'Real Threat' to Uzbek Security—Kazakh Paper," *BBC Monitoring Central Asia Unit*, based on report in *Karavan* [Almaty], March 1, 2002.

[248] "Tajik Drug Trade Thriving in Northern Afghanistan and Tajikistan," *Monitor*, January 22, 2002.

Afghanistan. If that is so, and assuming that the IMU has retained some of its connections in Afghanistan, the organization likely has not lost the narcotics phase of its financial underpinning. (Other drug trafficking organizations remain active in the region and could be responsible for the increased traffic in 2002.)

Trafficking in human beings, another criminal activity linked with international organized crime organizations, has increased significantly in Kyrgyzstan, mainly because of deteriorating economic conditions. According to United Nations official Ercan Murat, in 2001 human trafficking became the second most lucrative form of commerce in that country. It was ahead of tourism and behind only narcotics trafficking.[249] In 1999 an estimated 4,000 Kyrgyz women and girls were sold as prostitutes in the United Arab Emirates, Turkey, China, and Europe.[250] The role of Islamic militant groups in that activity has not been documented.

Hizb-ut-Tahrir (HT)

A second Islamic organization, the Hizb-ut-Tahrir (also seen as Hizb-al-Tahrir and the full form, Hizb al-Tahrir al-Islami, to be shortened henceforth in this treatment as HT), has become the most widespread underground Islamic movement in Uzbekistan, Tajikistan, and Kyrgyzstan. Founded in 1953 by Palestinians in Jordan and Saudi Arabia, the HT espouses the doctrine of jihad in Central Asia that would lead to establishment of Islamic caliphates throughout the Muslim world. The HT is violently opposed to the Shia variety of Islam, which is followed by significant populations in Uzbekistan and Tajikistan.[251] The HT claims to be the one true path of Islam, and that all other radical Muslim movements will be proven wrong.[252]

Rashid calls the HT "probably the most esoteric and anachronistic of all the radical Islamic movements in the world today."[253] Although Rashid notes that the HT's doctrine "largely does not even address central issues of public concern in Central Asia," he judges that the HT sees Central Asia as ripe for takeover by its form of jihad.[254] The Central Asian phase of the movement, which was first identified in Uzbekistan in 1995, is centered in the Fergana Valley

---

[249] United Nations, Integrated Regional Information Networks, "Interview with U.N. Chief in Kyrgyzstan," August 28, 2001.
[250] Agence France Presse, "4,000 Kyrgyz Women, Kids Sold to Slavery," December 20, 2000.
[251] Rashid, *Jihad*, 123.
[252] Rashid, *Jihad*, 123-24.
[253] Rashid, "A Peaceful Jihad, but There Will Be War," *Daily Telegraph* [London], January 23, 2002.
[254] Rashid, *Jihad*, 115.

among educated urban youth.[255] The HT also has developed a substantial following among the rural poor in Kyrgyzstan, Tajikistan, and Uzbekistan, however.[256]

Like the IMU, the HT has been persecuted in Uzbekistan and Kyrgyzstan, where thousands of group members have been imprisoned. The HT is organized in secretive, small cells of five to seven members; only the cell chief has contact with the next level of the organization. Unlike the IMU, the HT's doctrine does not approve violent measures to gain political control in the Islamic world, relying instead on distribution of propaganda materials and personal contact to gain converts. However, Rashid warns that the young extremists who increasingly are attracted to HT may react to ongoing persecution by the Karimov and Akayev regimes (Uzbekistan began mass arrests of HT members in 1999[257]) by embracing terrorist activities like those of the IMU. Said one of Rashid's informants, "If the IMU suddenly appears in the Fergana Valley, HT activists will not sit idly by and allow the security forces to kill them."[258] In October 2001, the HT website declared, "A state of war exists between [the United States] and all Muslims."[259] Rashid reports that some HT members were trained by the Taliban in Afghanistan and were in contact with IMU troops in 2001.[260]

The transformation of the HT into a terrorist organization would be a dangerous event in Central Asia for several reasons. First, HT's secretive and decentralized structure makes its activities very hard to track. Second, the HT has many more members than the IMU (an estimated 60,000 in Uzbekistan and 20,000 each in Kyrgyzstan and Tajikistan). The HT also has set up offices and proselytized successfully in the United Kingdom and Germany. Third, the chief of the national security forces of Kyrgyzstan has claimed that the HT's propaganda activities against the Kyrgyz government are funded by laundered money from narcotics sales, aided by al Qaeda's having "placed the well organized drug trafficking in their [HT's] service."[261]

There is little documentation of present HT narcotics activities. According to Rashid, the substantial funding behind HT's well-organized education and indoctrination programs comes

---

[255] Cornell and Spector.
[256] "Wanted Uzbek Islamic Leader May Be Still Alive—Kazakh Paper."
[257] Vitaliy Ponomarev, "Islom Karimov against Hizb al-Tahrir," report by Memorial Human Rights Center (Moscow), December 19, 2001.
[258] Ahmed Rashid, "A Peaceful Jihad, but There Will Be War," *Daily Telegraph* [London], January 23, 2002.
[259] Quoted in Adam Karatnycky, "Bush's Uzbekistan Test," *Christian Science Monitor*, March 13, 2002, 9.
[260] Rashid, *Jihad*, 133.
[261] Januzakov.

mainly from diaspora Muslims, notably those in Saudi Arabia and Western Europe. However, Rashid speculates that some HT cells are engaging in narcotics sales, using the same infrastructure as the IMU and other trafficking organizations in the region.[262] Presumably, HT's adoption of violent tactics against one or more Central Asian regimes would constitute a new linkage between organized crime and terrorism.

The IMU has strong reasons to follow the same pragmatic pattern with the HT as it followed with the Taliban in the late 1990s: alliance with a group that is different in ethnicity, origin, and overall goals, when a common enemy and common support networks are identified. Increasingly, the IMU and the HT have a shared identity as victims of repressive Central Asian regimes, whose rhetoric and enforcement strategy has been essentially the same for both groups. In 1999 the Uzbekistan government accused the HT of responsibility for an assassination attempt against Karimov, justifying a wave of arrests that followed. From that time, the Karimov regime and that of President Askar Akayev of Kyrgyzstan have lumped together the HT and the IMU as terrorist organizations and enemies of their respective states, and the groups have shared the abysmal prison conditions and human rights violations resulting from that status.[263] Both groups have reacted to the recent arrival of U.S. troops in Central Asia with strong anti-American rhetoric.

CONCLUDING POINTS

- Ahmed Rashid makes the very cogent point that the IMU is likely to continue as a major terrorist group as long as Central Asian governments prevent the existence of a legal political opposition.

- Given the dim prospects that outside pressure will push the Akayev and Karimov regimes toward toleration of dissent and the equally dim prospects for reducing Central Asian narcotics trafficking, the IMU is likely to remain a major connection between international narcotics and regional terrorism.

- The HT presents the potential for a second major linkage between narcotics and terrorism in Central Asia, although no major activity by HT has been documented in either area.

---

[262] Personal communication from Ahmed Rashid, March 21, 2002.
[263] Ponomarev.

- Alliance by the HT with the terrorist IMU would depend in part on how literally HT leaders understand their organization's claim to have the only answer to Islamification of the governments of Central Asia. As has occurred in numerous other cases, a strict adherence to that claim by HT could keep the groups separate in spite of their common goals and enemies, especially in light of rumors IMU is paying some of its followers for their loyalty. However, temporary alliances still could be justified.

- Any break by HT from its nonviolent methodology surely will reinforce existing support from al Qaeda. The large population of HT followers in two key countries along those routes, Tajikistan and Kyrgyzstan, and especially the spread of the movement into poor rural areas of those countries, gives HT cells easy access to narcotics profits as needed.

SELECTED BIBLIOGRAPHY

Cornell, Svante E., and Regine A. Spector. "Central Asia: More than Islamic Extremists," *The Washington Quarterly*, 25, No. 1, 193-221.

Olcott, Martha Brill, and Natalia Udalova. "Drug Trafficking on the Great Silk Road: The Security Environment in Central Asia," Carnegie Endowment for International Peace, *Working Papers*, No. 11, March 2000.

Rashid, Ahmed. *Jihad: The Rise of Militant Islam in Central Asia*. New Haven and London: Yale University Press, 2002.

Rashid, Ahmed. *Taliban: Militant Islam, Oil, and Fundamentalism in Central Asia*. New Haven and London: Yale University Press, 2000.

THE ABU SAYYAF GROUP (ASG)

Key Points

- The Abu Sayyaf Group (ASG), also known as the al Harakat-ul al Islamiyya (AHAI), is an Islamic fundamentalist secessionist group that seeks complete religious and political independence for the predominantly Muslim island of Mindanao, also known as the Autonomous Region of Muslim Mindanao (ARMM).

- ASG involvement in narcotics is limited to the sale and production of methamphetamine hydrochloride and marijuana, although kidnapping for ransom remains the group's primary source of financial support.

- Abu Sayyaf connections to narcotics trafficking developed out of an already rampant drug trade in Southeast Asia's Golden Triangle.

- The primary source of the ASG's international connections stems from founder Abdurajak Janjalani's service in the Afghan war. Janjalani's affiliations with Osama bin Laden (and therefore the al Qaeda network), 1993 World Trade Center bomber, Ramzi Yousef, and al Qaeda member Mohammad Jamal Khalifa (bin Laden's brother-in-law) were all forged during the Afghan war.

Background

Both the ASG and the Moro Islamic Liberation Front (MILF) are radicalized offshoots of the Moro National Liberation Front (MNLF), the Philippines' original Moro insurgent secessionist group. Of the three separatist groups operating in the Philippines, the ASG, literally "Bearer of the Sword," is the smallest. Also known as Al-Harakatul Islamia, the ASG is the only group that is not currently negotiating peace with the Philippine government. The ASG was established in 1989 as a result of disagreements with the MNLF over its reconciliation talks with the Philippine government about the establishment of a Muslim autonomous region.

Although MNLF leader Nur Misuari managed to maintain the loyalty of most of his group, the ASG's breaking away was not the first time that the MNLF had suffered a separation. In 1980 Hashim Salamat, a former leader of the MNLF, left that organization and founded the MILF. Similar to the ASG, the MILF's primary objective was the establishment of an entirely separate Islamic state.[264] Differing with the ASG and the MILF on this issue, in 1996 Nur Misuari signed a peace accord with the Philippine government in which the MNLF agreed to cease its insurgent activities. In return, and as a result of negotiations begun in 1989, Misuari's MNLF was granted control over the

region of the Philippines now known as the ARMM (Autonomous Region in Muslim Mindanao).[265] Because of the significance of

the ARMM to the economic health of the country, however, the Philippine government will be reluctant to grant independence to any secessionist groups in Mindanao. The ARMM is of particular importance to the Philippines because it makes up a significant part of the economic base of the Philippine's domestic production in agriculture and goods (40 percent of domestic food production[266]).

The ASG and the MILF both operate inside and on the edges of the ARMM in the regions of Basilan, Tawi-Tawi, and Sulu. Both the MILF and the ASG advocate a completely independent Islamic Republic (MIR) as opposed to the ARMM, which is regionally governed with its own executive, legislative, and judicial branches but defers to the Philippine government on external matters. In addition to demanding an independent state, the ASG advocates Islamic fundamentalism, but the group's dedication to that objective is under question, and the ASG is currently best known for its violent kidnapping activities as a bandit group.

The ASG gained international notoriety for its raid on the Christian city of Ipil in Mindanao.

---

[264] Peter Chalk, "Separatism and Southeast Asia: The Islamic Factor in Southern Thailand, Mindanao, and Aceh," *Studies in Conflict and Terrorism*, 24, No. 4, 2001, 247.

[265] Christos Iacovou, *From MNLF to Abu Sayyaf: The Radicalization of Islam in the Philippines*, Institute of Defense Analysis, Greece, July 11, 2000. <http://www.ict.org.il/articles/articledet.cfm?articleid=116>

[266] "Country Briefing: Sorting out the South," *The Economist,* July 11, 2001.

During the attack, 53 people were killed, several banks emptied, 20 hostages taken, and the city burned to the ground.[267]

The Philippine government's inability to decide how to portray the ASG to the international arena indicates confusion over Abu Sayyaf's identity. The government characterized it first as a terrorist organization and then as an insurgent group of bandits. It appears likely that the government may be exaggerating the ASG threat in order to attract international attention and support in its attempt to eliminate the secessionist group.

Abdurajak Janjalani, ASG Founder

The ASG's primary founder, Abdurajak Abubakar Janjalani, was born into a Muslim-Christian family in Basilan on November 8, 1953. He attended Claret College in Isabela for a short time before taking a scholarship in 1981 from the Saudi Arabian government to study Islamic jurisprudence and Arabic at Ummu I-Qura in Mecca. During that time, he also trained in military fighting tactics in Libya and Syria, and participated in the Afghan war against the Soviet invasion.[268] Upon his return to the Philippines, he began to preach Islamic fundamentalism and Muslim separatism.[269] Janjalani was assisted in the formation of the ASG by two other separatists, Amilhussin Jumaani and Ustadz Wahab Akbar.

The ASG lost much of its ideological Islamic fundamentalist base after Abdurajak Abubakar Janjalani was killed in a firefight with Philippine police on December 18, 1989. His brother, Khaddafy Janjalani, subsequently assumed power. Unlike his brother, Khaddafy was not trained in Islamic fundamentalism but rather received his training in explosives, and as a result the political focus of the ASG has diminished significantly.

---

[267] International Policy Institute for Counter-Terrorism, *Abu Sayyaf Group* (viewed on April 1, 2002). <www.ict.org.il/inter_ter/orgdet.cfm?orgid=3>
[268] <http://www.spynews.net/AbuSayyafGroup-1.htm>
[269] <http://www.ict.org.il/inter_ter/orgdet.cof?orgid=3>

Structure of the ASG

Abu Sayyaf is organized in a loose cell formation that is ruled by a caliph, or Islamic leader and eight supporters. Combined, they make up the Minsupala Islamic Theocratic State Shadow government (MIT-SG), the executive body of the ASG.

To speak of the ASG as a unified force belies its fractured relationship. Since the death of Abdurajak Janjalani, and because the ASG operates in small cells around the Philippines, there appears to be little coordination among groups. Further complicating the issue of unity and membership, there is evidence that the MILF and MNLF (despite the 1996 peace accord) are aiding the ASG in their kidnapping and terrorist efforts. However, both groups deny official support and cite instead the likelihood of "lost commands" (radicalized cells that do not follow the central command) engaging the ASG.

Support for the ASG's fundamentalist fervor is strongest in the poorest segments of Mindanao. The general unrest of the country's poorest, combined with the monetary incentives the ASG provides for cooperation, ensures substantial but erratic support. Reports indicate that the ASG recruits from the MILF, MNLF, and local citizens through payoffs secured through ransom.[270] Consequently, the membership of the ASG swells and contracts significantly according to the group's ransom bounties. Current estimates place the membership at between 1,500 and 4,000 participants.[271]

Recent Philippine military reports indicate that the MILF, the MNLF, and the ASG are establishing stronger ties to present a unified Muslim front in the quest for control of the ARMM. Reports indicate that the U.S. military training presence in the Philippines may be inciting the coalition. However, it is also possible that the Philippine government is seeking stronger control over the ARMM by using the perceived threat of a widening radical fundamentalism as a means of gaining support for its eradication of the entire secessionist movement.

---

[270] Armand N. Nocum, "Security Threat Raised as 5,000 MNLF Fighters Join Abu Sayyaf," *Manila Philippine Daily Inquirer* (Internet version), September 12, 2000.
[271] "Kidnapping Crisis: Groups Behind Abductions in the Philippines," as cited by *Jane's Intelligence Review* [London], January 12, 2001.

Foreign and Domestic Financial Influence in the Abu Sayyaf

The ASG receives its financial support primarily through kidnapping for ransom, but is increasingly involved in the sale of marijuana and methamphetamine hydrochloride, also known as *shabu*. In addition, some reports indicate that Abu Sayyaf receives a significant amount of financial backing from Islamic terrorist networks worldwide. The money is said to be funneled through semi-legitimate charity organizations based in Manila.[272]

Kidnapping for Ransom

The ASG is most notoriously known for its aggressive kidnapping of foreign tourists visiting the Philippines and Malaysia. In recent years, the ASG has significantly stepped up its kidnapping-for-ransom activities to finance its operations. The ASG's captives include the American couple Martin and Gracia Burnham, who were kidnapped from the island resort of Paliwan on May 27, 2001, and remain as hostages of Abu Sayyaf member Ismilon Hapilon.[273]

Although the Philippine government espouses a no-ransom policy, it does not interfere in ASG negotiations with foreign countries seeking the release of hostages. The ASG has secured millions of dollars—often referred to as "boarding fees"—through kidnapping, and has employed the help of the Libyan government as well as Hong Kong Triad members of 14-K to negotiate and transfer the funds.[274]

Most notably, the ASG used pre-established connections with the 14-K drug ring for the transfer of ransom funds from the Malaysian government in the case of the kidnapping of civilians from the Malaysian resort island of Sipadan in April 2000. The 14-K drug ring has been instrumental in assisting the group in obtaining ransom monies from Malaysia through an unnamed Chinese businessman named "Black Dragon."[275]

---

[272] Joshua Kurlantzick, "Fear Moves East: Terror Targets the Pacific Rim," *The Washington Quarterly*, 24, No. 1, 2000, 24.

[273] Jane Perlez, "Philippine Clashes May Point to Attempt to Rescue Hostages," *The New York Times,* March 25, 2002, A10.

[274] Donna S. Cueto, "Philippine Police Officer Links Abu Sayyaf to DrugTrafficking," *Manila Philippine Daily Inquirer* (Internet version), July 17, 2000.

[275] Alexander Young, "Ransom for Malaysian Hostages' Researse Said Paid Via Drug Links," *Philippine Star* (Internet version), July 20, 2000.

Drug Trafficking in Marijuana and Methamphetamine Hydrochloride

According to at least one report from Philippine intelligence, the ASG is increasingly relying on drug trafficking and sales for its financial backing.[276] Although most of the marijuana sold in the Philippines is produced and sold by local drug dealers and ASG members, the product is increasingly being exported to Australia.[277] Philippine intelligence indicates that the ASG grows much of its marijuana on the islands of Jolo and Basilan. [278] The group also has confirmed links to the Hong Kong Triad 14-K drug ring that provides Abu Sayyaf with arms from Hong Kong in exchange for assistance in the trafficking of *shabu* in the Philippines.[279]

The trail of trafficking for methamphetamine hydrochloride begins in the Philippines where the drug is produced and used domestically. The precursors for the drug are generally smuggled out of China by use of sea routes directly to the Philippines.[280] A report from the *Manila Pilipino Star Ngayon* indicates that members of the Philippine government permit the drugs–for–arms trade to continue because of pressure exerted by an unnamed Chinese businessman influential in the 14-K drug ring. Police corruption and involvement in the drug trade in the Philippines was corroborated in a hearing held by a Philippine investigation group in September of 2001, when a former narcotics agent testified to Philippine Senator Penfilo Lacson's involvement in drug trafficking with the Hong Kong Triads.[281]

Aid from International Sources

Libya has been consistent in its support for all Moro secessionist groups in the Philippines. In 1991, Libya sent part of an estimated P12 million in direct funding to the ASG.[282] In addition, aid has been donated from 1999 onwards for infrastructure projects and for the building of mosques in the impoverished southern Philippine areas.[283] There are suspicions

---

[276] Xinhua News Agency, "Abu Sayyaf now in Drug Trafficking," *Xinhua News Agency,* March 13, 2002. <http://news.xinhuanet.com/English/2002-03/13/content_314164.htm>

[277] International Narcotics Control Board, *Report of the International Narcotics Control Board for 2001,* United Nations Publication 2001, 48. <http://www.incb.org/e/ar/2001/menu.htm>

[278] Cueto.

[279] Cueto.

[280] International Narcotics Control Board, 2001.

[281] Christine Avendano, "'Rosebud' Links Lacson to Murder, More Crimes," *Manila Philippine Daily Inquirer,* September 4, 2001. <FBIS-EAS-2001-0904>

[282] Ron Gunaranta, "The Evolution and Tactics of the Abu Sayyaf Group," *Janes Intelligence Review* (online version), 2002.

[283] Lawrence Cline, "The Islamic Insurgency in the Philippines," *Small Wars and Insurgencies* [London], 11, No. 3, Winter 2000, 115.

that some kidnapping cases in which the Libyan government has paid ransom actually serve as a method through which Libyan financial support for the ASG is conducted. Negotiations are generally organized by Seif al-Islam, one of the sons of the Libyan leader, Colonel Mu'ammar Abu Minyar al-Qadhafi. Libya and Malaysia have also provided relief funds to help refugees in Mindanao.[284]

ASG direct links to al Qaeda and Osama bin Laden appear to have been dormant since 1995. Founder, Abdurajak Janjalani, became involved with bin Laden and al Qaeda in Afghanistan while fighting in the Afghan war. When Janjalani returned to Mindanao to establish the Abu Sayyaf, start-up monies were reportedly provided by private charity organizations under the care of bin Laden's brother-in-law, Mohammad Jamal Khalifa (most notably the International Islamic Relief Organization (IIRO) and the World Muslim League (WML)).[285] Thirteen of such organizations are currently under investigation by the Philippine government for their connections with domestic insurgent forces, such as the Abu Sayyaf. Peter Chalk, an analyst at the Rand Corporation, indicates that the ASG could have also received as much as P20 million through these institutions to fund travel and training for Abu Sayyaf militants in Peshawar.[286]

Terrorist Organizations and Links to Abu Sayyaf
Al Qaeda

The Philippine military and police are resolute in their confirmation that the ASG has direct links to the al Qaeda terrorist network. Research indicates that the initial relationship between the ASG's Abdurajak Janjalani and al Qaeda was substantial during the group's foundation in the early 1990s, both through Janjalani's participation in the Soviet-Afghan War and his subsequent connections with World Trade Center bomber Ramzi Yousef. Yousef, a personal colleague of Janjalani, trained ASG and MILF militants in explosives in 1994. He later

---

[284]Yael Shahar, *Libya and the Jolo Hostages,* August 20, 2000, International Policy Institute for Counter-Terrorism. <www.ict.org.il/articles/articledet.cfm?articleid=126>
[285] P. Parameswaran, "Philippines Pursues Money Trail of Bin Laden-Linked Abu Sayaaf," *Manila Phillipine Daily Inquirer* (Internet version), September 25, 2001.
[286] Chalk.

sought refuge with the ASG in the Philippines after the 1993 World Trade Center bombing and was eventually apprehended in Pakistan.[287]

Lost Commands

Because of the loose cell organization structure of the secessionist groups, the relative isolation these commands suffer, and the continued fracturing of MILF and MNLF support, renegade members of secessionist groups often form their own divisions of troops often called 'lost commands.' One such group is known as the Pentagon Group.

As early as 2001, the Philippine military identified a new kidnapping-for-ransom group made up of former MILF members calling themselves the Pentagon Group. Several incidents indicate that the Pentagon group maintains links with the ASG, and that the two operate in tandem to frustrate the Philippine military forces.[288]

Other International Links

Insurgent Moro groups such as the ASG have long shared a working relationship with the Libyan government from which it has received financial support for the construction of mosques and schools in the Philippines. More recently the Libyan government has introduced itself as a mediator in the negotiations between the Philippine government and its Muslim insurgent groups. In the case of the Sipadan kidnapping off the coast of Borneo in April 2000, the Libyan government provided the ransom monies to free four of the hostages being held, one of whom was a French-Lebanese woman.[289]

Abu Sayyaf also has indirect ties with the regional Muslim group Jemaah Islamiya (JI) in Indonesia. JI member, Fathur Rohman al Ghozi, also a colleague of Osama bin Laden, has established links with the MILF, and the two groups were complicit in conducting the bombing of a light rail system in December 2000.[290] Because the MILF and the MNLF are believed to coexist relatively peacefully together in Minadanao, and because evidence exists that

---

[287] Simon Reeve, *The New Jackals: Ramzi Yousef, Osama Bin Laden and the Future of Terrorism* (Cambridge, MA: Northeastern University Press, 1999), 135-136.

[288] Manila Times, "'Pentagon' Gang New Military Force in Mindanao: Villaneueva," *Manila Times Online,* August 23, 2001.

[289] International Policy Institute for Counter-Terrorism, *Libya and the Jolo Hostages,* August 20, 2000. <www.ict.org.il/articles/articledet.cfm?articleid=126>

[290] Fe Zamora, "Bin Laden Keeps 'Invisible' Links Among Local Muslims," *Manila Philippine Daily Inquirer* (Internet version), September 20, 2001.

Mohammad Jamal Khalifa has funded both the MILF and the ASG, it is likely that the ASG has direct links to the MILF and its subsequent networks. Reports from the Philippine military indicate that part of the difficulty in apprehending Abu Sayyaf militants is their ability to blend in with civilians and MILF group members. Military officials are reluctant to enter into ARMM-controlled areas where MNLF and MILF groups could be mistaken for Abu Sayyaf. The possibility of violating the 1996 peace accord between the Philippine government and the MNLF by military engagement between the two renders the capture of ASG members more difficult.[291]

There have been allegations that, in November 2001, MNLF leader Nur Misuari engaged the Abu Sayyaf directly in an attempt to prevent the loss of governorship over the ARMM and despite the 1996 peace accord. Misuari is currently being held in Kuala Lumpur on charges of violating the accord.[292]

CONCLUDING POINTS

- The current relationships with Hong Kong and Chinese drug rings in arms and narcotics dealings will most likely strengthen significantly as kidnapping for ransom becomes more risky.

- Current ASG chief Khaddafy Janjalani's leadership fails to encompass the ideological scope and strength of his late brother Abdurajak Janjalani's vision. As a result of the lack of ideological focus and the influx of large sums of ransom money into the cell network, the ASG is fracturing into its regional affiliations.

---

[291] Doug Struck, "Some Filipinos Cite Threats Beyond Abu Sayyaf," *The Washington Post,* March 4, 2002, A13.
[292] Norman Bordadora, "Manila Furnishes Malaysia Evidence Confirming Nur Misuari's Ties to Abu Sayyaf," *Manila Philippine Daily Inquirer (*Internet Version), November 27, 2001.

SELECTED BIBLIOGRAPHY

Chalk, Peter. "Separatism and Southeast Asia: The Islamic Factor in Southern Thailand, Mindanao, and Aceh," *Studies in Conflict and Terrorism*, 24, No. 4, 2001, 247-254.

Chalk, Peter. "Southeast Asia and the Golden Triangle's Heroin Trade: Threat and Response," *Studies in Conflict and Terrorism*, 23, No. 2, 2000, 89-106.

Cline, Lawrence. "The Islamic Insurgency in the Philippines," *Small Wars and Insurgencies* [London], 11, No. 3, Winter 2000, 115-138.

Gloria, Glenda M. "Morass in Mindanao," *The Irrawaddy* [Chang Mai, Thailand], 8, No. 7, July 2000, 1-3.

Iacovou, Christos. "From MNLF to Abu Sayyaf: The Radicalization of Islam in the Philippines," *International Policy Institute for Counter-Terrorism*, July 11, 2000. <www.ict.org.il/articles/articledet.cfm?articleid=116>

International Narcotics Control Board. *Report of the International Narcotics Control Board for 2001*. United Nations Publications, No. 2001. <http://www.incb.org/e/ar/2001/menu.htm>

Karmon, Ely. "Osama bin Laden: Speculations on Possible State Sponsorship," *International Policy Institute for Counter-Terrorism*, September 17, 2001. <www.ict.org.il/articles/articledet.cfm?articleid=385>

Kurlantzick, Joshua. "Fear Moves East: Terror Targets the Pacific Rim," *The Washington Quarterly,* 24, No. 1, Winter 2001, 19-29.

Reeve, Simon. *The New Jackals: Ramzi Yousef, Osama Bin Laden, and the Future of Terrorism*. Cambridge: Northeastern University Press, 1999.

Shahar, Yael. "Libya and the Jolo Hostages," *International Policy Institute for Counter-Terrorism*, August 20, 2000. <www.ict.org.il/articles/articledet.cfm?articleid=126>

Shahar, Yael. "Tracing bin Laden's Money: Easier Said Than Done," *International Policy Institute for Counter-Terrorism*, September 21, 2001. <www.ict.org.il/articles/articledet.cfm?articleid=387>

Ulph, Stephen. "Fears that Philippine Terrorist Group Is on the Rise," *Jane's Islamic Affairs Analyst* [London], October 2000, 1.

Yom, Sean. "Abu Sayyaf in the Philippines: More than Just Criminal," *CSIS Prospectus* (Center for Strategic and International Studies), 2, No. 3, Fall 2001. <http://www.csis.org/pubs/prospectus/01fall_yom.htm>

APPENDIX

Profile of the Revolutionary Armed Forces of Colombia (Fuerzas Armadas Revolucionarias de Colombia—FARC)[293]

Main Objective

❖ To overthrow the ruling order in Colombia and eliminate what it perceives to be U.S. imperialism in Colombia and elsewhere in Latin America.

Political Affiliation

❖ The FARC was adopted as the military wing of the Communist Party of Colombia in April 1966.

Insurgent Alliances

❖ There is some coordination of strategy with the ELN under the banner of the Simón Bolivar National Guerrilla Coordinator (Coordinadora Nacional Guerrillera Simón Bolívar—CNGSB).

Method of Funding/Criminal Activity

❖ The FARC engages in kidnapping and ransom, extortion, and drug trafficking. Foreign employees and their families in particular are vulnerable to kidnapping.

❖ Juan Pablo Rubio Camacho, a key FARC financial officer and money launderer, was captured in Bogotá in late March 2001. He had control of a Panamanian bank account of $50 million, which came from drug trafficking. In the previous 10 months, he had visited the FARC's *despeje* more than 100 times to confer with the FARC Secretariat. He also made frequent trips to Panama and Mexico.[294]

Domestic Links

❖ There are known links among the FARC, the ELN, and the drug cartels based in Colombia.

---

[293] Based in part on "Revolutionary Armed Forces of Colombia," Jane's World Insurgency and Terrorism Website, March 25, 2002. <http://www.janes.com>
[294] Claudia Rocío Vásquez R., "Capturado cerebro financiero de las Farc," *El Tiempo*, March 11, 2001.

Membership and Support

- ❖ The FARC is the largest left-wing organization in Colombia, having between 7,000 and 15,000 armed combatants plus a support base of another 10,000 people.
- ❖ Although the leaders are upper- and middle-class intellectuals, the fighters are largely rural-based peasants.

Area of Operation

- ❖ The FARC is rurally based but does have at least one urban wing. The FARC stages occasional operations over the Colombian border in Ecuador, Panama, and Venezuela.

Foreign Bases/Supply Lines

- ❖ The Soviet Union acted as a line of supply to the FARC before the end of the Cold War. The FARC still receives some support from Cuba and makes use of bases in Venezuela, Ecuador, and Panama, all of which are important routes for trafficking drugs and importing weapons. FARC members have at times sought sanctuary in northwestern Brazil.

Weapons/Arsenal

- ❖ The FARC uses M60 machine guns, M16 rifles, AK-47 assault rifles, mortars, RPG-7 rocket-propelled grenades, M79 grenade launchers, land mines, explosives, and detonators.
- ❖ Colombian National Police have confiscated AK-47s, HK G-3s, A-3s, Armalite-15s, Dragunov sniper rifles, Galil rifles, .50 calibre machine guns, 40mm grenade launchers, and C-90 grenades. Specifically, in 2000, they seized 45,000 firearms and 41,622 assorted caliber rounds of ammunition. The general weapon types confiscated were: 25,000 revolvers, 13,106 pistols, 5,114 shotguns, 161 carbines, 138 machine guns, and 232 rifles (not all specifically earmarked for FARC). In May 2000, Colombian officials also stopped at the border 50,000 AK-47 assault rifles, M60 machine guns, anti-aircraft and anti-tank rockets, R-15 and Galil rifles, and grenade launchers that were specifically earmarked for FARC. In addition, there have also been reports that FARC has, in the past, received SA-14, SA-16 and RPG-7s from Russia, as well as 'Redeye' and 'Stinger' missiles from Syria.[295]

---

[295] "FARC: Finance Comes Full Circle for Bartering Revolutionaries," Jane's Terrorism & Security Monitor Website, January 6, 2001. <http://www.janes.com>

Sources of Weapons

❖ During the Cold War, the FARC's weapons came from the Soviet Union and Cuba. Since then, they have been purchased on the international market from the Russian mafia and Central American arms dealers, or stolen from the Colombian military.

❖ By 1999 the FARC was obtaining large quantities of sophisticated weapons from Russian mafia sources in Eastern Europe.[296]

❖ The results of an investigation by the Brazilian Parliamentary Investigative Commission (CPI), released in January 2001, revealed that there is considerable competition among organized crime groups to supply weapons to the FARC via the Brazilian-Colombian border.[297] Automatic weapons, handguns, rifles, and even ground-to-air missiles are sent to the FARC via this route. According to the CPI, two major suppliers of weapons to the FARC are the Paraguayan Don Papito Cartel and the former Surinamese dictator Desi Bouterse. Carlos Castaño, leader of the right-wing paramilitary group Autodefensas Unidos de Colombia (AUC,) first exposed a Surinamese gun route after a shipment of weapons originally destined for the AUC was sold instead to the FARC. Castaño revealed the details of the transactions, naming a Brazilian businessman and owner of several airstrips, as the middleman, and "Jaime Angel" (who Castaño ordered to be killed) as the direct exchange contact. The CPI report, however, names Jorge Manuel Spricigo as the weapons purchaser and also implicates Leonardo Dias Mendona, one of Brazil's largest drug lords. Accounts also vary as to the origin of the weapons: Castaño reportedly claimed they were Chinese, but the CPI report states that they were American and Russian arms purchased on the black market. The weapons were flown into Brazil and then into Colombia. The Brazilian route is vulnerable, however, because at least eight unregistered aircraft were shot down crossing the Colombian-Brazilian border in 2000.

❖ The FARC purchases significant amounts of weaponry with significant amounts of cocaine.

---

[296] Douglas Farah, "Colombian Rebels Tap E. Europe for Arms," *Washington Post*, November 4, 1999, A1, A31.
[297] "FARC: Finance Comes Full Circle for Bartering Revolutionaries," Jane's Terrorism & Security Monitor Website, January 6, 2001. <http://www.janes.com>

Tactics/Methods of Operation

❖ The FARC remains committed to a long-term strategy of gaining power in the countryside until it is ready to capture Bogotá. It is becoming increasingly evident that the FARC and ELN can be defeated only militarily, which the Colombian government is incapable of doing.

❖ The FARC is the best equipped, trained, and organized insurgent organization in Latin America. Employing a wide range of tactics, it directly confronts the security forces in rural areas, maintains urban terrorist cells, and places bombs at strategic locations, such as oil installations and pipelines.

❖ Improvements in the FARC's military capabilities became evident beginning in 1996. The FARC command, headed by its military chief, Jorge Briceño ("Mono Jojoy"), completed a profound overhaul of FARC tactical procedures as a result of military training of FARC commanders in various East European military schools in the 1980s and assistance from advisors who were former Central American guerrillas. Operational innovations have included streamlining lines of command and control over units, thereby allowing for greatly improved ability to ambush government troops; introducing special forces to stage surprise attacks; and greatly increasing the firepower and lethality used to attack fortified installations.

❖ The FARC is also deeply involved in numerous criminal activities, including kidnapping and extortion (particularly directed at expatriates and foreign companies), and not only has links with the Cali and other drug cartels but is now believed to be directly involved in the production of cocaine.

❖ According to General Fernando Tapias, commander of the Colombian Armed Forces, the FARC's objective is to strengthen its urban war effort, for which   it needs new strategies and technology

Command Structure

❖ In the jungle regions, the FARC is divided into fronts; guerrilla activities are usually undertaken by no more than 150 fighters. Acts of urban terrorism are undertaken by city-based small cells.

Leadership

- ❖ Since its official inception in May 1966, the FARC has operated under the leadership of Pedro Antonio Marín (aka "Manuel Marulanda Vélez;" or "Tirofijo"–Sure Shot) (see photo), who is a FARC founder and its undisputed commander in chief.
- ❖ Hard-line military leader Jorge Briceño Suárez ("Mono Jojoy") is second in command of the FARC; commander, Eastern Bloc of the FARC; and, since April 1993, member, FARC General Secretariat.

Recent FARC International Connections

- ❖ Peruvian TV revealed a Colombian intelligence report alleging new links between Venezuelan President Hugo Chávez and the FARC. It claims that a Venezuelan colonel traveled to Colombian territory before the peace talks broke down to discuss two goals with FARC leader Manuel Marulanda: "First, to establish links for operations and negotiations with kidnapped individuals and with those who could potentially be kidnapped; and second, the possible displacement of the guerrillas to Venezuela."[298]
- ❖ *El Tiempo* reported on August 19, 2001, that the FARC has contact with the Russian, Ukrainian, Croatian, and Jordanian mafias, among others, which supply weapons and communications systems; and with armed groups in at least 18 countries.
- ❖ Three members of the Irish Republican Army (IRA)—James Monaghan (the IRA's head of engineering), Niall Terence Connolly (Sinn Fein's official representative in Havana), and Martin McCauley (an engineering and explosives expert) (see photo)—were arrested on August 11, 2001, as they left

---

[298] "Colombian report suggests links between Venezuela's Chavez, FARC," BBC Monitoring Service [UK], March 10, 2002, citing *El Espectador* Website, March 8, 2002.

a FARC-controlled area. They are accused of training FARC guerrillas in the use of Semtex explosives and traveling on false passports, but they claimed to be tourists.

❖ As many as 25 Irish Republicans might have spent time with the FARC. Two other Republicans who were in Colombia when Niall Connolly, Martin McCauley, and James Monaghan were arrested escaped via Venezuela and are back in Ireland. According to Ireland's *Evening Herald*, citing the Colombian secret police, Monaghan and McCauley were training rebels in the construction of an antipersonnel mine known locally as a "Chinese hat".[299]

❖ *La Tercera* [Santiago, Chile] reported on March 14, 2000, that the FARC is supporting Chile's Arauco-Malleco Coordinator of Communities in Conflict (Coordinadora de Comunidades en Conflicto Arauco-Malleco), which is the most radical branch of the Mapuche insurgent movement.[300]

Method of Funding

❖ The FARC's annual income has been estimated as high as US$500 million.

❖ FARC is now involved in sophisticated money laundering schemes using Colombian banks. The laundered money is in accounts that are available electronically.

❖ The FARC is heavily involved in numerous criminal activities, including kidnapping and extortion (particularly directed at expatriates and foreign companies).

❖ The FARC not only has links with the Cali and other drug cartels but is now believed to be directly involved in the production of cocaine.

FARC Communications Technology

❖ A *Jane's* analyst has attributed the success of the narco-terrorists in Colombia to an unlimited source of income, as well as to their expertise in the areas of diplomacy, strategy, organization, improvisation, intelligence collection, weapons and demolitions, computer technology, advanced secure communications systems, the ability to identify political, economic and military objectives, the ability to select and train leaders, and to make superior use of both the Colombian and U.S. legal systems.[301]

National Liberation Army (Ejército de Liberación Nacional—ELN)[302]

Front Organization

❖ The ELN operates a series of factions and fronts, including the Camilo Torres Restropo, the José Antonio Galán, the Alfred Gómez, the moderate Corriente de Renovación Socialista, and the Domingo Lain Sanz (the most radical faction). The centralist faction, formerly led by the late Manuel Pérez, is the largest. The most important faction is the Simón Bolivar faction, which opposes the more hardline elements of the ELN.

---

[299] David Sharrock, "Up to 25 Republicans' with Colombian Rebels," *The Daily Telegraph* [London], January 8, 2002, 10.

[300] Fredy Palomera, "Investigan nexos de mapuches con las Farc," *La Tercera de la Hora* [Santiago], March 14, 2000.

[301] Gregory A Walker, "Combatting a Criminal Insurgency," *Jane's International Police Issues*, December 3, 1998.

[302] Based on information from Rob Fanney, "National Liberation Army (Ejército de Liberación Nacional—ELN)," January 25, 2002.

Objectives

- ❖ The ELN's principal aim is to "seize power for the people" and establish a revolutionary government.
- ❖ The ELN is more politically motivated than FARC and is strongly nationalistic. It particularly opposes foreign-owned oil companies.

Political/Religious Affiliation

- ❖ The ELN's doctrine is based on a mixture of Maoism and Marxism, but is also heavily influenced by Fidel Castro.

Date of Founding

- ❖ July 4, 1964

Insurgent Alliances

- ❖ The ELN attempts to co-ordinate strategy with the other major Colombian groups under the banner of the Simón Bolivar National Guerrilla Coordinator (Coordinadora Nacional Guerrillera Simón Bolívar—CNGSB).
- ❖ The ELN works directly with FARC and has had links with the Tupac Amaru Revolutionary Movement (Movimiento Revolucionario Tupac Amaru—MRTA) in Peru.

Rival Insurgent Groups

- ❖ Colombian United Self-Defense Groups.

Method of Funding

- ❖ The ELN engages in extortion and kidnapping. It also obtains funds from the drug trade through locally imposed revolutionary taxes.

Membership and Support

- ❖ Membership is drawn from across Colombian society, including students, left-wing middle and upper class intellectuals, and peasants. It therefore has both a rural and an urban support base.
- ❖ Total membership is probably about 3,000 combatants.

Area of Operation

- ❖ The ELN operates primarily in the north and northeast of the country, including the border region of Venezuela.

Foreign Bases/Supply Lines

❖ The ELN still receives some support from Cuba and makes use of bases in Venezuela, Ecuador, and Panama, all of which are important routes for trafficking drugs and importing weapons.

Weaponry/Arsenal

❖ M16 rifles, AK-47 assault rifles, RPG-7 rocket-propelled grenades, land mines, explosives, and detonators.
❖ Two surface-to-air missiles (SAMs) were seized in September 1998 by the Colombian Army.

Sources of Weapons

❖ Purchased on the international market, or stolen from the military. According to an advisory board for national security, 90 percent of the ammunition used by the guerrillas belonged to the Venezuelan military; most of it was sold by members of the Venezuelan Army.

Tactics/Methodology

❖ ELN actions include bombings of oil pipelines and oil installations, kidnapping, and guerrilla warfare.

Command Structure

❖ The ELN is divided into various factions, the most active of which operate in rural areas in fronts led by a local commander.
❖ The group has suffered from a lack of strong, centralized leadership.

Leadership

❖ Ricardo Lara Parada and Fabio Vásquez led the group into the 1970s; since then, factionalism has plagued the group. Of the more prominent members, Francisco Galén is still in prison and Manuel Pérez died in February 1998.

United Self-Defense Forces of Colombia (Autodefensas Unidas de Colombia—AUC)

Aims/Objectives

❖ To counter the influence of left-wing guerrilla organizations

Political Affiliation

❖ Right-wing

Date of Founding

❖ The core of the AUC was founded in the mid-1990s, but the paramilitaries really arose from the right-wing death squads of the 1980s, many of which were employed by landowners.

Insurgent Alliances

❖ The AUC is an umbrella organization of likeminded paramilitary groups.
❖ Human rights groups have accused the government of links with the paramilitaries, and there is evidence of past collusion with the military.

Method of Funding

❖ The AUC taxes coca growers and demands extortion money for protecting drug facilities and crops. Some reports indicate that the AUC is also directly involved in cocaine exports.

Membership and Support

❖ Estimates vary. The number of members is believed to be between 8,000 and 13,000.

Area of Operation

❖ Llanos Orientales, César, Magdalena Valley, Santander, Casanare, Cundinamarca, the Pacific coast, south and southeast Colombia, and some urban cells. The groups also operate in the border areas with Panama, Ecuador, and Venezuela.

Foreign Bases/Supply Lines

❖ The AUC operates in the border areas with Panama, Ecuador, and sometimes Venezuela.

Weaponry/Arsenal

❖ Assault rifles, machine guns, explosives.

Sources of Weapons

❖ Locally available on the black market.

Command Structure

❖ Similar organization to other local guerrilla organizations, with AUC groups led by local commanders.
❖ There is co-ordination, political and strategic direction provided by the Autodefensas Campesinas de Córdoba y Urabá (ACCU) leadership.

Leadership

- ❖ Fidel and Carlos Castaño founded the ACCU in the mid 1990s; both were trained by the military to act as death squad leaders. Carlos Castaño resigned in 2001, but is understood to still run the AUC's political activities.
- ❖ The AUC claims that it has at least 35 retired military officers serving with the organisation.

Background

- ❖ Using the organizations that had been established by the military as death squads during the 1980s, the Peasant Self-Defense Groups of Córdoba and Urabá (Autodefensas Campesinas de Córdoba y Urabá—ACCU) was established in the mid-1990s.
- ❖ Increasingly individual death squads and paramilitary groups came together under an umbrella organization, believed to have informal links with the Colombian military.
- ❖ The groups targeted left-wing guerrilla organizations and civilians accused of assisting them, as well as becoming increasingly involved in the narcotics trade.

Shining Path (Sendero Luminoso—SL)[303]

Front Organization

- ❖ The SL was originally a faction that split from the Peruvian Communist Party Red Flag group under the leadership of Abimael Guzmán Reynoso. Following the arrest of Guzmán and his subsequent call to relinquish arms, two rejectionist factions emerged: Red Sendero (Red Path) and Perú Rojo (Red Peru).

Objectives

- ❖ To destroy existing institutions in Peru and replace them with a peasant revolutionary regime that would rid the country of foreign influences.

Ideology

- ❖ Political doctrine is based on a mixture of the ideologies of Marx, Lenin, Mao, and Abimael Guzmán Reynoso (SL's founding leader).

Date of Founding

- ❖ 1969.

International Connections

- ❖ Evidence exists of links with Spain's Euzkadi Ta Askatasuna (ETA) and the Abu Nidal Organization (ANO).

---

[303] Based on information from Brian Marshall, "Sendero Luminoso," Jane's World Insurgency and Terrorism Website, January 17, 2000. <http://www.janes.com>

Method of Funding

❖ Funding comes primarily through drug trafficking, kidnapping for ransom, bank robbery, and extortion, including the raising of "revolutionary taxes."

Membership

❖ An estimated 300 members.

Area of Operation

❖ Some attacks have been made in Lima. Since 1995, actions have been concentrated in areas from which the Peruvian Army had been redeployed to the border with Ecuador.

Weapons

❖ The SL has reportedly stolen an estimated 1 million tons of mining explosives. The SL inventory also includes AK-47 and FN rifles, rocket-propelled grenades, and handguns. Weapons are obtained from the regional black market or stolen from the Peruvian security forces.

Tactics/Methodology

❖ Urban terrorist activity has been directed against the diplomatic missions of almost every country represented in Peru, including the embassies of the former Soviet Union and the Peoples's Republic of China. Foreign businesses, symbols of government, and humanitarian projects have all been attacked.

Organization

❖ The SL has traditionally been divided into four sections: Armed Propaganda, Sabotage, Selective Killings, and Guerrilla Warfare. Red Sendero is divided into several columns, each of about 200 guerrillas. Information on the organization of Red Peru is unavailable.

Leadership

❖ In September 1999, a Peruvian newspaper identified Filomeno Cerrón Cardoso ("Artemio"), leader of the Huallaga Regional Committee, as the new SL leader following the arrest of Oscar Ramírez Durand. Artemio was reported to be allied with the drug traffickers in the coca-producing Huallaga Valley.

LEBANON

Profile of Hizballah[304]

Alias/Front Organisation

❖ Party of God, Revolutionary Justice Organisation, Organisation of the Oppressed on Earth, Islamic Jihad for the Liberation of Palestine. Founded in 1983, Hizballah assumed most of the apparatus and remaining personnel from the 1980s umbrella coalition of groups known as Islamic Jihad. The guerrilla wing in Lebanon is Islamic Resistance (IR).

Aims/Objectives

❖ To establish a radical Shia Islamic theocracy in Lebanon, ensure the destruction of the state of Israel, and eliminate all Western influences from the region.

Religious Affiliation

❖ Radical Shia Islam.

Insurgent Alliances

❖ Hizballah is wary of alliances with other guerrilla organisations. In Lebanon, it has worked with Amal, although the two are political rivals. The Amal breakaway organisation, Islamic Amal, led by Hussein Musawi, has been incorporated into Hizballah. Hizballah provides some training facilities for Hamas and Palestinian Islamic Jihad, and it has placed some suicide bomb trainers in Palestinian-held territory since the beginning of the Al Aqsa Intifada in October 2000. The group is mistrustful of outsiders and in general considers most Palestinian groups to be riddled with informants. Hizballah-International, through its leader Imad Mughniyah, is linked with some Al-Qaida leaders. In Latin America, Hizballah has a strategic relationship with the Revolutionary Armed Forces of Colombia (FARC) organisation.

Rival Insurgent Groups

❖ Until Israel's withdrawal from southern Lebanon in May 2000, any Israeli-backed militia organisation was the main focus of Hizballah's guerrilla activities. Although it forms alliances with radical Sunni or non-Islamic revolutionary organisations, the group's Shia heritage ultimately makes any of these groups a rival.

Method of Funding

❖ Iran is believed to donate funds to Hizballah; some estimates claim that these are in the region of US$60 million annually (exact figures are unknown). The group also collects donations from individuals and charities, and benefits from legitimate commercial enterprises. There is evidence that Hizballah receives funds from narcotics, both cultivation and smuggling in Lebanon and elsewhere. Its presence in the tri-border area

---

[304] Based on information from "Groups: Hizbullah," Jane's World Insurgency and Terrorism Website, March 25, 2002. <http://www.janes.com>

between Argentina, Paraguay, and Brazil (see below) brought links with known international criminals such as Ali Khalil Merhi, arrested on charges of fraud and music and software piracy. Merhi is also believed to have channelled funds into the cells responsible for terrorist activities against Israeli targets in Argentina in 1992 and 1994. Hizballah's so-called strategic alliance with FARC in Colombia also raises the likelihood of narcotics funding, and the group was involved in negotiations by the Iranian government to build a refrigeration plant in FARC-held territory in San Vicente del Caguan, Colombia. (This project was abandoned under pressure from Washington.)

Commercial Fronts

❖ Hizballah has direct business interests in Lebanon, Iran, Latin America, and elsewhere. It is involved in a variety of activities, including construction, foodstuffs, and clothing manufacture.

Charitable Fronts

❖ The group's welfare and educational programmes are run by charitable foundations, which collect money, often quite legitimately, from Shia communities inside and outside Lebanon. The "Organisation of the Oppressed on Earth" acts as a charity and welfare organisation.

Membership and Support

❖ There are thousands of non-combatant members of Hizballah; estimates of military strength are more difficult to determine. Sources concerning IR's strength vary. There is believed to be a core of around 300 to 500 elite fighters and another group of Hizballah guerrillas numbering between 3,000 and 5,000 who are not all full-time insurgents. Some sources claim that there are 15,000 reservists.

Area of Operation

❖ Hizballah operates in southern Lebanon, where it is the de facto security apparatus in the absence of any real government security presence in the region. IR has bases in the Beka'a Valley and a support network amongst the Shia villages in the south. The group also maintains a strong political presence in other major cities, but particularly in Beirut. It has offices and training facilities in Iran and possibly Sudan. Hizballah has training facilities on the Isla de Margarita off the northerncoast of Venezuela and a strong presence in the tri-border area around the towns of Cuidad del Este in Paraguay, Foz de Iguazu in Brazil, and Puerto Iguazu in Argentina. Regional intelligence suggests that the perpetrators of the 1992 attack on the Israeli Embassy and the 1994 attack on the Jewish Cultural Centre in Buenos Aires were harbored among the large Lebanese community in this region.

Foreign Bases/Supply Lines

❖ Hizballah is assisted by Syria, the Syrian military apparatus, and the pro-Syrian Lebanese government. Supplies of arms and equipment are airlifted from Iran into Damascus airport, where they are transferred to southern Lebanon by Syrian forces. Since 1999, some supplies have been flown directly into Beirut.

Weaponry/Arsenal

* ❖ IR operates a number of M113 APCs, and guerrillas are usually armed with M16 or AK-47 assault rifles and an assortment of other weaponry, including Bangalore torpedoes, hand grenades, AT-3 "Sagger" and AT-4 "Spigot" anti-tank missiles, Western-designed TOW anti-tank missiles, and rocket-propelled grenades. The IR has also reportedly taken delivery of a range of air defence weapons, including Strela-2 (SA-7) surface-to-air missiles, as well as ZU-23 anti-aircraft (AA) guns, and 57 mm AA guns. Fire-support teams are equipped with 81 mm and 120 mm mortars, 106 mm recoilless rifles, and short- and long-range 122 mm Katyusha rockets; IR was reported to have obtained two Soviet-made towed 122 mm guns in the late 1990s, and in May 2000 is believed to have seized some of the tanks and APCs that were abandoned when the South Lebanon Army (SLA) collapsed. Other reports of deliveries from Iran since late 1999 may have included the Russian KBM Igla (SA-18 "Grouse") man-portable low-altitude surface-to-air missile system. Since 1999 the group has reportedly been using photocell technology to detonate sophisticated roadside bombs.

Sources of Weapons

* ❖ Hizballah receives weaponry mainly from Iran; some weapons were seized from the SLA in May 2000.

Tactics/Methodology

* ❖ One of the primary aims of Hizballah was to expel the Israeli military from southern Lebanon; to this end, it mounted ambushes on Israeli and SLA units in southern Lebanon, and attacked into northern Israel itself, using Katyusha rockets. IR relies on a sophisticated intelligence and counter-intelligence capability, assisted by Iranian and Syrian intelligence; the latter is believed on occasion to have penetrated Israel's own intelligence capabilities, allowing Hizballah to launch surprise attacks. The group concentrated on undermining the morale of Israeli soldiers posted to southern Lebanon and of civilians living in areas of northern Israel targeted by Hizballah's Katyushas, so that the war in southern Lebanon became politically unpopular. The group has maintained pressure on the Israeli military over the disputed Sha'aba Farms area, still occupied by Israel.

Training

* ❖ IR guerrillas are reckoned to be amongst the most dedicated, motivated, and highly trained of their kind. Any Hizballah member receiving military training is likely to do so at the hands of Iranian Revolutionary Guards, either in southern Lebanon or in camps in Iran. The increasingly sophisticated methods used by IR members indicate that they are trained using Israeli and U.S. military manuals. The emphasis of this training is on the tactics of attrition, mobility, intelligence gathering, and night-time maneuvers.

Command Structure

❖ Hizballah is more than a guerrilla organisation. It is a political, social, welfare, commercial, and educational network. The ruling body of the organisation is the Higher Consultative Council, and there are three regional councils based in Beka'a, Beirut, and South Lebanon. IR is a small, highly effective guerrilla organisation trained and directed by Iranian Revolutionary Guards. IR commanders do not necessarily inform Hizballah's Higher Consultative Council about strategy. Hizballah's overseas network is even more secretively run. Known loosely as Hizballah-International, it is directed by Imad Mughniyah.

Leadership

❖ One of the organisation's original founders, Sheikh Abbas Moussawi, led Hizballah and IR until February 1992, when he was killed by the Israelis. His role as Secretary General was assumed by Sheikh Hassan Nasrallah, considered more moderate than his predecessor but without the level of influence within IR. Imad Mughniyah, one of the most wanted men in the world, heads Hizballah-International. He is believed to be living in Iran.

Political Wing

❖ Hizballah operates as a legitimate political party in Lebanon, participates in elections, and hold seats in the National Parliament.

Communications

❖ Hizballah's command, control, and communications are among the most sophisticated of any guerrilla group. Its operatives have used the Internet as well as their social and welfare programmes to promote their message. The organisation's web site is frequently the target of cyber attack by Israel.

Level of Threat

❖ Hizballah poses a very significant threat to Israeli and U.S. interests. Hizballah's military campaign in southern Lebanon effectively defeated Israel; its relentless and bloody tactics are widely believed to be the reason for the May 2000 unilateral withdrawal from most of the area (there is still a dispute over the status of the Sha'aba Farms). The group also has a formidable international wing, which in the past has committed significant terrorist attacks, and the leader of Hizballah-International, Imad Mughniyah, remains one of the world's most wanted men.

ALBANIA AND MACEDONIA

Profile of the National Movement for the Liberation of Kosovo and Kosovo Liberation Army (KLA or UCK)[305]

Aims and Objectives

❖ Secession by the province of Kosovo from the Federal Republic of Yugoslavia and unification with Albania.

Political and Religious Affiliation

❖ Muslim; ethnic Albanian nationalism.

Date of Founding

❖ Constituent groups have been active since 1995.

Status

❖ Under the terms of the agreement reached with the Federal Republic of Yugoslavia, the NATO-led peace force was mandated to disband the KLA. In 1999 the KLA agreed officially to hand in weapons and become a legalized security force. However, after the formation of that force, the Kosovo Protection Corps, KLA elements have remained at large and beyond the control of the KLA political authorities.

Insurgent Alliances

❖ The groups have links with militias in Albania and with ethnic Albanian insurgent groups in Macedonia, including Unikom.

Rival Insurgent Groups

❖ KLA splinter groups have fought each other in northern Macedonia.

Funding

❖ Donations from sympathetic groups in Albania; the government also claims that there is Iranian influence within the organizations. Splinter groups in Macedonia have been identified with Balkans' narcotics and human trafficking.

Membership and Support

❖ Unknown, but an estimated 85 per cent of Kosovo's population are ethnic Albanians (known as Kosovars), and secession from Serbia is a popular cause.

---

[305] Based on information from Jane's World Insurgency and Terrorism Website, July 4, 2000 <http://www.janes.com>, and updated using various online accounts.

Area of Operation

❖ Serbian security forces have driven remaining KLA forces in Kosovo into the mountains, most of its fighters retreating to the border with Albania. KLA splinter units are almost certainly based in Albania and are active in Macedonia.

Foreign Bases and Supply Lines

❖ The groups are believed to have links in Albania.

Weaponry

❖ KLA forces reportedly were armed with Kalashnikov assault rifles, machine guns, explosives, artillery pieces and grenades.

Sources of Weapons

❖ Weapons and materials for bomb-making equipment were believed to be smuggled from Albania into areas of military activity, via sympathetic Albanians in Macedonia.

Tactics and Methodology

❖ After an ineffective terrorist campaign that concentrated on poorly protected Serbian police and civilian targets and which seemed to harm as many Kosovars as Serbs, in 1998 the group began an organized insurgency. This change in tactics threatened the balance of power in the Province and compelled the government in Belgrade to mobilize security forces to regain territory over which it had lost control.

Command Structure

❖ The KLA was organized and led by local commanders.

Leadership

❖ Brigadier General Agim Ceku is the former KLA chief of staff, currently commander of the Kosovo Protection Corps.

Political Wing

❖ After clandestine elections, Kosovars declared a "shadow" independent Republic of Kosovo with Ibrahim Rugova of the Democratic League of Kosovo becoming "president." He promoted a policy of passive resistance, which is opposed by the hardline Kosovan politician Adem Demaçi.

Level of Threat

❖ The activity of the remaining KLA groups in Northern Macedonia remains a problem in northern Macedonia, where the successor Albanian National Army seems to be a growing force. However, there is rivalry with former guerrilla groups in the region.

❖ Other separatist groups have emerged since the KLA officially disbanded, including the Liberation Army of Presevo, Medvedja, and Bujanovac (UCPMB, *q.v.*), founded by

Albanian separatists from three municipalities in southern Serbia. The group, which officially renounced military activities in May 2001, claimed to have no links with the KLA.

Profile of the National Liberation Army (Ushtria Çlirimtare Kombëtare, NLA or UCK)[306]

Alias/Front Organization

❖ The organization is also sometimes known by the initials UCK, for its Albanian language name, the Ushtria Çlirimtare Kombëtare. The organization is a distinct, separate entity from Yugoslavia's Kosovo Liberation Army guerrillas in Kosovo Province, whose Albanian name, Ushtria Çlirimtare ë Kosoves, also yields the acronym UCK.

Aims and Objectives

❖ The declared aim of the NLA is to retain Macedonia's unified state status, but with a new constitution and international mediation over ethnic Albanian grievances. The group's critics, however, allege that the real aim of the NLA rebels is to create a "Greater Albania" or a "Greater Kosovo," joining ethnic Albanian people from southern Serbia, Macedonia, Kosovo and possibly Albania.

Religious Affiliation

❖ Muslim.

Date of Founding

❖ The NLA emerged in late 2000, and has since swallowed up previous Albanian guerrilla groups in Western Macedonia, including Unikom. Various ethnic Albanian guerrillas have been active in Western Macedonia since the early 1990s.

Status

❖ No known activity since disarmament of August 2001, but known to retain substantial support among Albanian minority population in northern Macedonia. Part of NLA's structure merged into Coordinating Council of Albanians in Macedonia, founded to implement the 2001 Framework Agreement for Albanian rights in Macedonia. NLA leader Ali Ahmeti heads that council.

Insurgent Alliances

❖ NLA has welcomed former Unikom members as well as other ethnic Albanian guerrillas in Macedonia. It is allied to the remnants of the KLA (*q.v.*) in Kosovo and the UCPMB (*q.v.*) in southern Serbia.

---

[306] Based on information from Jane's World Insurgency and Terrorism Website, July 3, 2001 <http://www.janes.com>, and updated from a variety of online sources.

Rival Insurgent Groups

❖ There is evidence of Macedonian militia activity, from groups that include the Inner Macedonian Revolutionary Organisation (IMRO). Fighting reported in northern Macedonia between NLA and Albanian National Army forces, March 2002.

Funding

❖ The NLA received assistance from allied rebel groups and organizations in Albania and from Kosovo Province.

Membership and Support

❖ Membership included several hundred active members, some of whom are former Kosovo Liberation Army (KLA) guerrillas.

Area of Operation

❖ The NLA operated in western Macedonia. Guerrillas also used ruined Ottoman forts in Mount Baltepe, and the Sar mountains.

Foreign Bases and Supply Lines

❖ The NLA had bases in Albania and in Kosovo Province.

Weaponry

❖ The NLA's weapons included Kalashnikov assault rifles, machine guns, explosives, and grenades.

Sources of Weapons

❖ The NLA received its weapons from Albania and Kosovo Province.

Tactics and Methodology

❖ The organization's members engaged in sporadic clashes and hit-and-run ambushes against Macedonian security forces.

Command Structure

❖ Unknown.

Leadership

❖ The political leader is Ali Ahmeti, a native Macedonian, who was instrumental in the formation of the Kosovo Liberation Army (KLA) while living in exile in Switzerland. He is also a veteran of the war in Kosovo. Fazli Veliu, a well-known ethnic Albanian nationalist, was an important founder of NLA who is participating in the Coordinating Council.

Political Wing

- ❖ Folded into Coordinating Council of Albanians in Macedonia, under Ahmeti.

Level of Threat

Prior to the 2001 accord, the group was a small and not significant threat, but its political impact could be far greater than its military effectiveness. Most ethnic Albanians in Macedonia (between 25 and 40 percent of the population) harbor grievances against the government, and given the volatility of the region, even relatively small actors and events can have a huge impact.

Profile of the Liberation Army of Preševo, Medvedja, and Bujanovac (UCPMB)[307]

Alias/Front Organization

- ❖ N/A

Aims and Objectives

- ❖ The UCPMB sought the secession of three districts in southern Serbia having large Albanian populations: Preševo, Medvedja, and Bujanovac. There are disputes as to whether the rebels wanted a "Greater Albania" or a "Greater Kosovo," but the group did aim to create a state joining ethnic Albanian people from southern Serbia, Macedonia, Kosovo, and possibly Albania.

Political/Religious Affiliation

- ❖ Increasingly prominent Muslim influence.

Date of Founding

- ❖ The UCPMB emerged at the beginning of 2000, although many of its members had already fought in Kosovo.

Status

- ❖ Officially renounced military action, May 2001.

Insurgent Alliances

- ❖ The UCPMB was allied with the remnants of the Kosovo Liberation Army (KLA), the National Liberation Army (NLA) in Macedonia, and militia groups in Albania.

Rival Insurgent Groups

- ❖ Rivals of the UCPMB included extremist Serbian militias.

---

[307] Based on information from Jane's World Insurgency and Terrorism Website, July 3, 2001 <http://www.janes.com>, and updated with various online reports.

Funding

❖ The UCPMB raised funds via drug trafficking and organized crime from supporters in Albania and Kosovo, as well as local donations.

Membership and Support

❖ Estimates of UCPMB membership vary, but its numbers likely ranged from several hundred to 2,000 armed members. Wider support also existed among ethnic Albanians in southern Serbia.

Area of Operation

❖ The UCPMB operated in Presevo, Medvedja, and Bujanovac in southern Serbia, and across the border in Kosovo, from headquarters in Mali Trnovac and rear base at Gnjilane. Controlled Veliki Trnovac, a local center of narcotics and arms trafficking and prostitution. UCPMB activity also frequently spilled over into Western Macedonia and Albania.

Foreign Bases and Supply Lines

❖ The UCPMB has bases in and receives supplies from Albania, Kosovo, and Western Macedonia. In the past there have been accusations that Iran, Libya, and Islamist extremist groups such as al Qaeda also have fomented unrest in the region and provided guerrillas with funds.

Weaponry

❖ The UCPMB fielded Kalashnikov assault rifles, machine guns, explosives, artillery pieces, grenades, and landmines.

Sources of Weapons

❖ The UCPMB received weapons from local sources, and also from sources in Albania.

Tactics and Methodology

❖ The UCPMB staged attacks on Serbian civilian and police targets.

Command Structure

❖ Unknown.

Leadership

❖ Commander was Shefket Musliu.

Political Wing

❖ Political Council for Preševo, Medvedja, and Bujanovac, headed by Januz Musliu (cousin of military commander Shefket Musliu).

Level of Threat

- ❖ The group was small and not militarily strong; it is difficult to gauge its popularity with Albanians in southern Serbia, given its violent methods. The principal threat posed by the UCPMB lay in the ability of relatively small factors and actors to upset the status quo in the area, and create further instability, which might lead to wider fighting. The group claimed to have no links with the KLA.

CENTRAL ASIA

Profile of the Islamic Movement of Uzbekistan (IMU)[308]

Alias/Front Organization

❖ "Islamic Party of Turkestan (IPT)" was assumed as a name for a time in 2001 but later specifically repudiated by movement leaders.

Aims and Objectives

❖ To establish a radical Islamist "caliphate" from the Caspian Sea to Xinjiang in western China. The group's initial aim was to overthrow the Karimov government of Uzbekistan and establish an Islamist regime in that country.

Political and Religious Affiliation

❖ Radical Sunni Muslim; IMU recruitment offers of regular pay have drawn comments that some members are not motivated by religious fervor.

Date of Founding

❖ The group was founded in 1998, but leaders of the IMU had been active in opposition Islamic activities in Uzbekistan as early as 1991.

Status

❖ Active; membership depleted to an unknown degree by military defeats in Afghanistan in late 2001 and early 2002, but some outposts in Afghanistan and substantial outposts in Tajikistan and Kyrgyztan remained.

Insurgent Alliances

❖ Close ties have been formed with al Qaeda and the Taliban. Military leader Juma Namangani in particular has enjoyed the patronage of both organizations and in return has applied his forces to protect Taliban positions and act as couriers for narcotics being smuggled from Afghanistan into Central Asia. This axis has brought the IMU into alliance with a number of Islamist groups in Afghanistan, including Abu Sayyaf Group; Armed Islamic Group (GIA); Harakat ul-Mujahideen (HuM); Harakat ul-Ansar; Salafist Group for Call and Combat (GSPC); Libyan Islamic Fighting Group; Al-Itihad al-Islamiya (AIAI); Islamic Army of Aden/Islamic Army of Aden and Abyan, radical Palestinian groups, and elements of the Chechen rebel movement. The IMU's objectives with regard to Central Asia have brought a closer bond with ethnic Uyghur guerrillas from Xinjiang, western China, some of which have fought in IMU brigades.

---

[308] Based on information from Jane's World Insurgency and Terrorism Website, November 27, 2001 <http://www.janes.com>, and updated using reports from numerous online sources.

Rival Insurgent Groups

❖ The Northern Alliance Forces in Afghanistan, Jamaat e Islami; Jumbish-i-Milli (National Islamic Movement - NIM) and Hizb-i Wahdat-Khalili. Other anti-Taliban (hence implicitly anti-IMU) guerrilla groups in Afghanistan include Hezbi Islami Gulbuddin; Hizbi Islamic-Khalis; Ittihad-i-Islamic Barai Azadi Afghanistan; Harakat-Inqilab-i-Islamic; Jabha-i-Najat-i-Milli Afghanistan; Mahaz-i-Milli-Islami; Hizbi Wahdat-Akhari; Harakat-i-Islami and Hezbi-Wahdat, and the Shi'ia umbrella organization.

Funding

❖ The IMU has been given financial support by al Qaeda through a combination of commercial interests, Osama bin Laden's personal wealth, and charitable donations. The IMU's primary source of funding has been drug trafficking. Tensions are believed to have broken out between some Taliban leaders and the IMU over the Taliban's ban on opium production prior to its retreat in late 2001.

Commercial Fronts

❖ The IMU's integration with the al Qaeda network has enabled it to benefit financially from the business and financial fronts and backers associated with Osama bin Laden. These include commercial enterprises in the Middle East and North Africa, particularly in Yemen and Somalia, and some ventures in the West. The Barakat/Barakaat group of companies and the al-Taqwa group have been identified as likely benefactors to the terror network established by al Qaeda.

Charitable Fronts

❖ Charitable funding from Uzbekistan has been difficult to organize because the state tightly controls such activities. Mosques and religious institutions are closely monitored and closed down by the government if they come under suspicion. But charitable fronts elsewhere, particularly in Pakistan, have supplied the IMU as an ally of the Taliban and al Qaeda. The al-Rasheed Trust has been accused of smuggling weapons and supplies, disguised as humanitarian aid, to insurgents.

Membership and Support

❖ Estimates in 2001, before the U.S.-led military strikes against Afghanistan, put the strength of the armed branch at around 5,000. These forces were predominantly Uzbek, Kyrgyz and Tajik nationals, as well as ethnic Uzbek and Tajik Afghans. They were serving with some Pakistani and Slavic nationals and were given support in the form of safe houses by local Kyrgyz and Uzbek people.

Area of Operation

❖ Before the U.S.-led attacks on Afghanistan and advances by the Northern Alliance, the IMU was able to operate freely in all Taliban-held areas of Afghanistan, although most units were stationed along the borders of Uzbekistan and Tajikistan. The bulk of the fighting forces used Afghanistan as winter quarters, as well as supplementing Taliban units. They established a base in Tavildara in west central Tajikistan, and despite the presence of some 30,000 Russian troops in Tajikistan, the IMU operates in the inhospitable mountainous interior of the country. They have been known to infiltrate Uzbekistan, employing small, mobile units. In 2000, an incursion into Uzbekistan by 100 militants took them to within 62 miles of the capital, Tashkent. IMU units also are known to have infiltrated and established cells in southwestern Kyrgyzstan.

Foreign Bases and Supply Lines

❖ The most significant foreign base is in Tajikistan, centered around the IMU base at Tavildar. The group has a presence in the Tajik and Uzbek enclaves of southwesternmost Kyrgyzstan and in the Fergana Valley area, where opposition to the Uzbek government is strong. The IMU's links with Islamists in Tajikistan include Mirzo Ziyev, the Minister for Emergency Situations in the coalition government of Tajikistan. In the past, the IMU has also been able to make use of facilities in Pakistan. The IMU's assistance to Uyghurs fighting in western China also gives the group as presence in Xinjiang where ethnic similarities to Uyghurs make detection difficult.

Communications

❖ The IMU has access to the full range of sophisticated communications equipment available to al Qaeda and has used video tapes and literature to smuggle drugs into Central Asia. Since 1998 there has been a growing wariness among Afghan-based guerrillas about using the Internet and satellite telephones, which are tracked by U.S. and local intelligence services. Couriers have been used to convey messages, and the route between Afghanistan and into Central Asia and western China is well traveled by IMU drug traffickers.

Weaponry

❖ The IMU reportedly is armed with AK-47s, sniper rifles, night vision equipment, grenade launchers, pistols, and silencers.

Sources of Weapons

❖ Kalashnikov rifles and other infantry weapons are widely available from Pakistan and Afghanistan; some weapons are stolen and purchased from military units in Central Asia, including Russian units.

Tactics and Methodology

❖ In 1999 and 2000, the IMU undertook summer offensives into Uzbekistan, Tajikistan, and Kyrgyzstan, with the aim of expanding its bridgehead in the Central Asian republics and gaining control of the economically critical Fergana Valley. Movement into Kyrgyzstan was necessitated by Uzbekistan's strong security measures and pressure from the Tajikistan government to cease using bases in that country to attack Tajikistan's neighbors. The IMU also was responsible for seizing hostages, hit-and-run ambushes on army bases, and car bombings. In Afghanistan the IMU assisted over-stretched Taliban units in the north of the country against the Northern Alliance. In the wake of the

Taliban's retreat in late 2001, the IMU was expected to break into small infiltration units, which will "disappear" into Tajikistan to regroup and may take opportunities to carry out reprisals on Uzbek targets in particular.

Training

❖ The IMU has found a plentiful supply of recruits in the impoverished Fergana Valley area, many of whom were opposed to the repressive President Karimov. In Tajikistan, Uzbekistan, and Kyrgyzstan, young men are attracted by the regular pay, which, according to some sources, is about US$100 per month plus food and clothing (in an area where the average pay is US$1 per day). Volunteers have received military training and religious instruction at camps in Afghanistan run by the Arab 055 Brigade of al Qaeda. Most were trained in guerrilla warfare and sabotage, and some are believed to have been instructed in bomb making, assassination, and urban terror tactics.

Command Structure

❖ Exact command structure for the group is unclear; brigades are made up according to ethnic backgrounds but most infiltration work for guerrilla incursions or drug trafficking is undertaken by small units of around 15 men, under a commander who reports to an area commander. Joint operations have been carried out with al Qaeda and Taliban forces, and the military commander of the IMU also was appointed a joint "defense minister" for the Taliban. In the past, claims by the Taliban to be amassing troops on the border with Uzbekistan have in fact referred to IMU volunteers based in the north.

Leadership

❖ Chairman of the Supreme Council of the IMU is Zubair ibn Ahdurrahim, and the chief political and religious leader is Tahir Yuldashev. However the most high profile is Juma Namangani, the IMU military commander and one of the de facto defense ministers for the Taliban. Namangani is an ethnic Uzbek whose charismatic image has been compared to that of Che Guevara. According to some accounts, Namangani was killed in the U.S. campaign against the Taliban in late 2001, but no positive confirmation has been received. Yuldashev is known to remain in control of the political arm of the organization in early 2002.

Political Wing

❖ The adoption of the name the Islamic Party of Turkestan (IPT) may have been an attempt to widen the group's religious and political appeal in the Central Asian region. The Uzbek government has claimed that Hizb-ut-Tahrir, a very popular radical movement that promotes the establishment of a caliphate across much of Central Asia, is a front organisation for the IMU, although this is denied by Hizb-ut-Tahrir.

Level of Threat

❖ The IMU's threat to Central Asian stability has been exaggerated by some reports but, even before the 11 September 2001 attacks, the group was considered a potent and capable ally of al Qaeda. In 2000, the Clinton administration promised US$10 million in aid to help counter-insurgency operations for Kyrgyzstan, Uzbekistan and Tajikistan. The IMU poses a very significant threat to stability in Central Asia, where poverty is widespread and dissent is repressed harshly. Tajikistan has been wracked by civil war (although its coalition government has shown signs of viability); the authoritarianism of the Uzbek government is widely disliked; and Kyrgyzstan is impoverished and increasingly repressive. All these conditions make infiltration easier. In the wake of the U.S.-led military campaign against Afghanistan, the IMU is believed to have dissolved into small units that have taken refuge in Tajikistan and the Kyrgyz portion of the Fergana Valley. From those enclaves, such groups pose a threat to Uzbek, U.S., and Russian targets.

THE PHILIPPINES

Profile of the Abu Sayyaf Group[309]

❖ The Abu Sayyaf Group (ASG) was originally known as the Mujahideen Commando Freedom Fighters (MCFF), then al Harakat-ul al Islamiyya (AHAI), and now the ASG.

Aims/Objectives

❖ The ASG aims to establish an independent Islamic republic in Mindanao and surrounding islands. ASG also aims to eliminate other religions in the Muslim regions of the Philippines.

❖ The ASG is part of an international radical coalition opposed to the United States and its allies.

Leadership

❖ The ASG was founded by Philippine native Abdurajak Abubakar Janjalani, who studied Islamic law in Libya and fought in Afghanistan during the 1980s, and Amilhussin Jumaani and Ustadz Wahab Akbar, who studied in Iran and Syria.

❖ Ustadz Muhammad Hatta Haipe (Abu Abdel Aziz) is the ASG's secretary general. It's spokesperson is Abu Sabaya.

Insurgent Alliances

❖ The ASG's relationship with al Qaeda is considered so close that many analysts view the ASG as part of the al Qaeda network. Among those al Qaeda associates who have worked with the ASG are Ramzi Ahmed Yousef, a personal friend of Janjalani. The ASG assisted Yousef's visits to the Philippines and is suspected of involvement in a plot to assassinate the Pope when he visited Manila. A senior al Qaeda member, Jamal Khalifa, a Pakistani national who is Osama bin Laden's brother-in-law, is married to a Filipina and is al Qaeda's main liaison with the ASG.

❖ The link with al Qaeda and roots in Afghanistan have brought ASG members into contact with the Egyptian Islamic Jihad, the Taliban, Chechen Islamists, Armed Islamic Group (GIA), Harakat ul-Mujahideen (HuM), Harakat ul-Ansar, Islamic Movement of Uzbekistan (IMU), Salafist Group for Call and Combat (GSPC), Libyan Islamic Fighting Group, Al-Itihad al-Islamiya (AIAI), Islamic Army of Aden/Islamic Army of Aden and

---

[309] Based on information from: "The Abu Sayyaf Group," Jane's World Insurgency and Terrorism Website, 2001. <http://www.janes.com>

Abyan, Uighur separatists, and radical Palestinian groups, including Hamas and Palestinian Islamic Jihad.

❖ Philippines intelligence also claims that the ASG has criminal links with the Sri Lankan separatist Liberation Tigers of Tamil Eelam (LTTE), who sent combat trainers to ASG and MILF camps in the 1990s.

Membership and Support

❖ The ASG reportedly has at least 1,500 members, although some estimates range from a few hundred to 4,000.

❖ Most members are under 20 years old and recruited from the southern Philippines, in particular Patikul, Sulu, Lebak, Sultan Kudarat, Malapatan, Sarangani, and Zamboanga City. They are given financial incentives for joining, and members are paid for recruiting friends and relatives; citizens residing near ASG camps are also employed as scouts.

Images courtesy of http://www.Inq7.com (*Philippine National Inquirer*)

Area of Operation

❖ The ASG is located mainly in Basilan and Sulu provinces in Mindanao, but the group does maintain a wider presence in Zamboanga City, Cotobato City, Davao City, and Dipolong City.

Foreign Bases/Supply Lines

❖ At least until late 2001, Afghanistan and Pakistan hosted important training facilities, and liaison points for the ASG to meet with other radical organizations. These countries also served as sources of support, including supplying weapons.

❖ Smugglers based in Basilan, particularly those from Babuan and Lantawan, illegally import arms shipments for guerrillas in the area.

Weaponry/Arsenal

❖ The group is supplied with rifles, including AK-47s.

❖ Recent acquisitions are believed to include more sophisticated weapons, such as mortars, heavy machine guns, and grenade launchers.

Sources of Weapons

❖ Weapons are smuggled into the country, or bought from Hong Kong and China. There are also accusations that arms dealers in Vietnam and Malaysia are involved in the supply. Although the group has in the past received assistance from Libya, such assistance is thought to come in the form of training and direct financing rather than weapons and explosives.

Command Structure

❖ Guerrillas operate in small units under a single commander. Those with experience gained in Afghanistan are accorded greater seniority and respect.

❖ The secretary general is responsible for co-ordinating all military and operational activities.

❖ After Abdurajak Janjalani died in 1998, Commander Khaddafy and Abu Sabaya took over command of the Basilan group, which is the strongest of the ASG's forces.

❖ The Sulu area is commanded by Abu Jumdail (Dr. Abu), Galib Andang, and Mujid Susukan.

❖ The group has become increasingly factionalized; the Basilan group was greatly influenced by Janjalani and is viewed as more religiously motivated. The Sulu group has been criticised by the Basilan faction for concentrating on criminal activity at the expense of strategic goals.